The Economic Effects of
Surface Freight Deregulation

The Economic Effects of Surface Freight Deregulation

Clifford Winston

Thomas M. Corsi

Curtis M. Grimm

Carol A. Evans

The Brookings Institution | Washington, D.C.

Copyright © 1990 by
THE BROOKINGS INSTITUTION
1775 Massachusetts Avenue, N.W., Washington, D.C. 20036

Library of Congress Cataloging-in-Publication data:

The Economic effects of surface freight deregulation / Clifford
   Winston . . . [et al.].
     p.   cm.
   Includes bibliographical references.
   ISBN 0-8157-9468-1 (alk. paper)
    1. Freight and freightage—United States—Deregulation.
   I. Winston, Clifford, 1952–
   HE597.U6E26   1990
   388′.044—dc20   90-1962
                                                 CIP

9 8 7 6 5 4 3 2 1

The paper used in this publication meets the minimum requirements of
the American National Standard for Information Sciences—Permanence
of Paper for Printed Library Materials, ANSI Z39.48-1984.

Foreword

THE 1980 Motor Carrier Act and the Staggers Rail Act of 1980 largely deregulated the motor carrier and railroad industries. By opening the surface freight transportation industry to market competition, deregulation has led to significant changes in the way rates are set and in the rates shippers pay, in the service that is provided, and in carrier operations.

In this study Clifford Winston, Thomas M. Corsi, Curtis M. Grimm, and Carol A. Evans quantitatively assess the effects of surface freight deregulation on the welfare of shippers, motor carriers, railroads, and labor. They find that deregulation has substantially benefited shippers and railroads at some cost to the less-than-truckload segment of the motor carrier industry and to the rail and motor carrier labor force, for an annual net gain to the nation of nearly $16 billion (1988 dollars). Because the industry is still adjusting to deregulation, the authors identify how further increases in competition and operating efficiency can provide additional benefits to shippers and carriers. The authors recommend policies for the rail and motor carrier industries to further these objectives.

Clifford Winston is a senior fellow in the Brookings Economic Studies program; Thomas M. Corsi is a professor of business and management at the University of Maryland; Curtis M. Grimm is an associate professor of business and management at the University of Maryland; and Carol A. Evans is a former research assistant in the Brookings Economic Studies program. The authors are grateful to Scott Dennis and Peter French of the Association of American Railroads, to Leland Gardner, Kent Phillips, Les Selzer, and Walt Strack of the Interstate Commerce Commission, and to staff members at Brookings, the U.S. Department of Justice, the U.S. Department of Transportation, and the Federal Trade Commission for valuable assistance and comments. They also received thoughtful and constructive suggestions from Kenneth Boyer, Ronald Braeutigam, Andrew Daughety, John Due, Alfred Kahn, James MacDonald, Henry McFarland, and Thomas Moore. Discussions with Darius Gaskins, John Meyer, and Robert Willig were also helpful. Research assistance was provided by Judith L. Jarrell and Leslie Siddeley.

Brenda B. Szittya edited the manuscript, Roshna M. Kapadia verified its factual content, and David Rossetti provided staff assistance. The study was funded in part by a grant from the Alfred P. Sloan Foundation.

The views expressed in this book are those of the authors and should not be ascribed to those persons or organizations whose assistance is acknowledged or to the trustees, officers, or other staff members of the Brookings Institution.

BRUCE K. MAC LAURY
President

April 1990
Washington, D.C.

Contents

Tables

Figures

Chapter One

Introduction

AMERICA'S freight transportation system has undergone a great transformation during this century. Until the 1950s the railroads were the overwhelming mode of choice, transporting as much as three-quarters of the nation's intercity freight in 1929 and almost 70 percent as late as the end of World War II (table 1-1). By the 1960s the growth of the intercity trucking industry, spurred by the development of the interstate highway system in the mid-1950s, and the growing importance of such specialized forms of transportation as water and pipeline had put an end to the nation's heavy dependence on rail. Today, rail, truck, inland water transport, and pipeline are all vital components of the freight system.

The history behind these changes is familiar: technological change and public investment in highway and water infrastructure led to the emergence and growth of new modes of transportation, which, coupled with an expanding set of shippers' needs, led to a more even distribution of traffic among the modes. But an equally important part of the system's history involves government regulation, particularly of the rail and truck industries.[1]

Regulation of the railroad industry began with the Interstate Commerce Act of 1887, which created the Interstate Commerce Commission (ICC).[2] This legislation eased tensions between railroads and shippers and served what was perceived to be the public interest by requiring "reasonable and just rates" that did not exploit shippers because their size or location limited their bargaining power. It also stabilized the industry by averting

---

1. We do not include water carriers and pipelines in our analysis because water carriers were already largely deregulated before regulatory reform in the railroad and motor carrier industries began in the 1970s and because regulatory reform has not yet reached the pipeline industry in a sweeping manner.

2. For an influential discussion and critique of surface freight transportation regulation, see John R. Meyer and others, *The Economics of Competition in the Transportation Industries* (Harvard University Press, 1959). For recent summaries of freight transportation regulation, see Elizabeth E. Bailey, "Public Policy Appraisal: Two Hundred Years of Transportation and Communication Policy," Ameritech Distinguished Lecture Series, University of Illinois, March 1988; and Theodore E. Keeler, *Railroads, Freight, and Public Policy* (Brookings, 1983).

Table 1-1. *Modal Shares of Intercity Freight Ton Miles, Selected Years, 1929-88*[a]

			Mode			
Year	Rail	Truck	Great Lakes	Rivers and canals	Oil pipelines	Air
1929	74.9	3.3	16.0	1.4	4.4	0.0
1939	62.4	9.7	14.0	3.7	10.2	0.0
1944	68.6	5.4	10.9	2.9	12.2	0.0
1950	56.2	16.3	10.5	4.9	12.1	0.0
1960	44.1	21.7	7.7	9.2	17.4	0.0
1970	39.8	21.3	5.9	10.5	22.3	0.2
1975	37.3	21.7	4.9	11.9	24.0	0.2
1980	37.5	22.3	3.9	12.5	23.6	0.2
1987	36.8	25.1	2.8	12.8	22.2	0.3
1988	37.0	25.2	2.8	12.7	21.9	0.3

Source: Association of American Railroads, *Railroad Facts, 1977* and *1988* (Washington: AAR, 1977 and 1988); 1987 and 1988 figures from the Eno Foundation for Transportation, Inc., *Transportation in America, A Statistical Analysis of Transportation in the U.S.*, 7th ed. (Westport, Conn., May 1989), p. 7.

a. Includes both for-hire and private carriers.

rate wars, although it was not until the Transportation Act of 1920 that minimum rates could be legally set by ICC approval of industry proposals. Following World War II, the railroads' rate of return fell as they began losing traffic to trucks, barges, and pipelines.[3] The adverse effects of regulation then became apparent: railroads were unable to adjust their rates in a timely fashion to changing market conditions; they were unable to shed unprofitable portions of track, thus incurring higher capital and maintenance costs; and they were unable to consolidate and integrate their networks effectively to improve their service.[4] The railroads' problems are typical of those that occur when government assumes responsibilities that the market would ordinarily assume. The railroads' inability to abandon excess trackage, for example, left thousands of miles of track and related facilities that became the railroads' equivalent of obsolete military bases.

Despite shedding unprofitable intercity rail passenger service by selling it to a quasi-public corporation (now called Amtrak) created by Congress

3. Association of American Railroads, *Railroad Facts, 1988* (Washington, November 1988), p. 18.

4. *Improving Railroad Productivity: Final Report of the Task Force on Railroad Productivity*, A Report to the National Commission on Productivity and the Council of Economic Advisers, Washington, November 1973 (John R. Meyer, Chair of Task Force).

in the Rail Passenger Service Act of 1970, the railroads' financial problems continued, culminating in the 1970s with the bankruptcies of several Northeastern and Midwestern railroads and with nearly every railroad earning a rate of return below that earned in the corporate sector as a whole. Regulation had put a stranglehold on the industry that was preventing it from competing effectively.[5] Congress dealt with the immediate problem of the bankruptcies of the Penn Central and other Northeastern railroads through the passage in 1973 of the so-called 3R Act (Regional Rail Reorganization Act). The act set up the United States Railway Association to plan the reorganization of the bankrupt railroads and to administer federal funds provided in the legislation for branch line subsidies, for protecting rail labor affected by any recommended restructuring, and for upgrading passenger service on the Northeast corridor. Three years later the 4R Act (Railroad Revitalization and Regulatory Reform Act) infused billions of dollars into Conrail, the name given to the portion of the bankrupt Northeast rail system judged to be viable, and provided funds for Northeast corridor passenger service and subsidies for branch lines and commuter rail service.[6]

As the words "regulatory reform" in the title of the 4R Act indicate, Congress recognized the importance of fundamental changes in regulation as part of the solution to the railroads' problems. However, the actual regulatory reforms in the bill, especially as implemented by a cautious ICC, were insufficient to remove the array of regulatory burdens crippling the railroads.[7] Finally, in 1980, consistent with its unfolding approach to problems in other regulated industries, Congress chose to deregulate the railroad industry in a direct, unambiguous fashion. The Staggers Rail Act of 1980 directed railroads to return to profitability by relying on the market.

Government regulation of trucking also led to undesirable results, but in different ways. In 1935, spurred by strong lobbying by railroads fearful of growing motor carrier competition, Congress enacted the Motor Carrier Act and gave the ICC authority over truck rates and entry into markets.[8]

---

5. See the references in note 2. Other factors such as high labor costs, restrictive work rules, and low managerial quality also contributed to rail's financial problems. For a discussion, see United States Railway Association, *Final System Plan*, vol. 1 (Washington, July 26, 1975).

6. Frederick J. Stephenson, Jr., *Transportation USA* (Addison-Wesley, 1987), pp. 115–16, provides a full discussion of the 3R and 4R Acts.

7. Robert C. Lieb, *Transportation*, 3d ed. (Prentice-Hall, 1985).

8. Congress specifically exempted the transportation of unprocessed agricultural goods

Initially, motor carrier rates for regulated commodities were patterned after rail charges. Where their service advantage existed, motor carriers could attract traffic from rail with equal rates. In the early years after 1935, however, roads were too poor and trucks too small to allow the trucking industry to divert much traffic from the railroads. During the 1950s two developments accelerated the diversion of traffic from rail to truck. The first and most important was the construction of the interstate highway system, which greatly shortened the travel time between major metropolitan areas. The improved roads also made possible the use of larger trucks, which were able to carry heavier loads and thus reduce the cost of transporting freight. The second development was the emergence of a highly competitive unregulated trucking sector consisting of owner-operators (self-employed truckers) who carried exempt commodities, and private trucking (firms primarily engaged in other activities shipping their freight in their trucks).

Although the regulated trucking industry became quite profitable, it too became the target of congressional deregulation. This time the object of Congress and the ICC was not to improve financial performance, but to lower rates, especially in the less-than-truckload (LTL) sector. (This trucking sector specializes in transporting shipments of less than 10,000 pounds using break-bulk terminals in the context of a hub-and-spoke route system.) Various studies concluded that the trucking industry's collective ratemaking system, composed of regional rate bureaus, resulted in rates in the LTL sector that were considerably higher than they would be in a fully competitive environment.[9] To remedy this situation, Congress passed the Motor Carrier Act of 1980, which substantially deregulated the regulated trucking sector by limiting collective ratemaking, easing entry restrictions, and encouraging pricing freedom. It also opened the industry to even greater competition by allowing (unregulated) private trucking firms, which had been forbidden to carry other firms' freight, to transport freight from

---

from regulation as a concession to the powerful agricultural interests. See Lieb, *Transportation*, p. 263. ICC jurisdiction over domestic water carriers was given by the Transportation Act of 1940; over oil pipelines, by the Hepburn Act of 1906. The Federal Energy Regulatory Commission took over responsibility for regulating pipelines in 1977.

9. For one example, see John W. Snow, "The Problem of Motor Carrier Regulation and the Ford Administration's Proposal for Reform," in Paul W. MacAvoy and John W. Snow, eds., *Regulation of Entry and Pricing in Truck Transportation* (American Enterprise Institute, 1977), pp. 3–46.

wholly owned subsidiaries of their parent company. (Private trucking firms had already been given the ability to solicit freight as for-hire carriers by the ICC Toto Purchasing and Supply Company decision in 1978.)[10]

The deregulation of the rail and trucking industries represents a major turning point in the evolution of the surface freight transportation system. Its effects, however, have been a source of public controversy, with cries for reregulation emanating from various quarters. This book provides a comprehensive evaluation of the economic effects of the deregulation legislation on shippers, on railroads and trucking firms, and on the labor force in the two industries. It also recommends additional policies that can improve industry performance and identifies areas where further deregulation would be beneficial.

In the analysis that follows, we find that surface freight deregulation has been extremely beneficial to shippers and to their customers. Total annual benefits from rate and service changes amount to $20 billion, with each mode contributing net benefits. (These results and all succeeding figures in this chapter are in 1988 dollars.) Deregulation has also enhanced railroad industry profitability by $2.9 billion annually. The truckload (TL) sector of the trucking industry has benefited slightly. But the LTL sector of the trucking industry has lost $5.3 billion in profits annually from deregulation. And the number of LTL trucking jobs has fallen, as have LTL and railroad workers' wages. Thus, surface freight deregulation has, on net, benefited the American economy, while redistributing wealth from labor and one segment of the motor carrier industry, the LTL carriers, to consumers and railroads.

Even greater benefits to shippers are attainable, but at the cost of radical redistribution. If deregulation resulted in rates that were equal to marginal cost, shippers would gain an additional $10.2 billion annually. Railroads, however, would stand to lose nearly that amount. For an industry that has not earned a normal rate of return for fifty years, redistribution on such a scale would threaten its very survival.

Because the freight transportation industry is still adjusting to its new regulatory environment, we expect further efficiency improvements, leading to lower rates and higher rail profitability. We recommend that policymakers carefully monitor these changes and for the time being take only fairly minor steps consistent with the thrust of deregulation. In the

10. *Toto Purchasing and Supply Co., Inc.* 128 MCC 873 (March 24, 1978).

event that shipper benefits or rail profitability seriously deteriorates, we recommend a contingency policy, which would entail separation of rail operations and ownership of the infrastructure. The premise underlying all our policy proposals is that the benefits from deregulation can only be enhanced if policymakers continue to promote efficiency and competition among carriers.

Chapter Two

Regulatory Policy and Rail and Motor Carrier Operations

DEREGULATION of surface freight transportation was prompted on economic grounds by vast inefficiencies caused both by rate and by entry and exit regulation. When the railroads were first regulated at the end of the nineteenth century, rates were set, in principle, according to the value of the commodity shipped. This policy served the interests of farmers and homesteaders by ensuring low rates for their commodities. As time progressed, rail and motor carrier rate structures became more complex and could not simply be characterized by "value-of-service" price discrimination. Kenneth Boyer, for example, found that regulated motor carrier rates during the early 1970s were consistent with cartel ratemaking yet were highly responsive to the bargaining power of high-volume shippers.[1] Indeed, cartelization was legally sanctioned by the 1948 Reed-Bulwinkle Act, which gave the trucking industry antitrust immunity to set rates collectively in regional rate bureaus. Boyer also found that regulated railroad rates had a value-of-service component but were also strongly influenced by ICC efforts to follow the spirit of the 1887 Interstate Commerce Act and prevent undue rate discrimination by size and location.

Market entry and exit regulations for the two industries differed from the beginning. Incumbent motor carriers were given operating certificates for their existing routes. Entry by new carriers or by existing carriers into new markets was permitted only if the carrier could justify its entry on the grounds of "public convenience and necessity." Any authority that was granted specified the commodities that could be hauled and the routes along which each commodity could be carried.[2] Operating authority could be denied if incumbent carriers made a case that entry would hurt them

---

1. Kenneth D. Boyer, "Equalizing Discrimination and Cartel Pricing in Transport Rate Regulation," *Journal of Political Economy*, vol. 89 (April 1981), pp. 270–86.
2. This practice led to classifications of ICC-regulated motor carriers as irregular route and regular route common carriers. Irregular route carriers could haul only certain commodities between specified origins and destinations but were free to establish their routings. Regular route carriers had to follow specific routings between their origins and destinations.

financially or if they decided to offer the proposed service. Although applications for new interstate carrier certificates grew steadily following the onset of regulation, the number of such carriers actually declined gradually.[3]

Given the maturity of the rail industry by the time it was regulated and the enormous capital requirements for entry, entry regulation was not a significant consideration. But exit regulation was important. Railroads were discouraged from abandoning routes by a lengthy and costly application procedure. Further, the ICC usually did not approve an abandonment request in the face of shipper or local government opposition.

The political basis for the different forms of regulatory "protection" is easy to identify. The main thrust of railroad exit regulation was to prevent railroads from abandoning service to communities that had it; the communities effectively outvoted the railroads, which was fine with the politically potent railroad unions. In the case of the trucking industry, the Teamsters were an ally in lobbying for a vast network of entry restrictions, which served their interests, not the communities', and the interests of the less-than-truckload carriers that primarily employed them.

Costs of Regulation

The costs of these regulations to society turned out to be substantial. Two major distortions are frequently cited and quantified in the literature: first, rates were held above marginal costs for both modes; and, second, entry and exit restrictions substantially raised carriers' costs. Rate distortions cost society roughly $1 billion annually.[4] (Distortions in the case of trucking were worse in the less-than-truckload sector, where shippers had no recourse to the private carriage and rail alternatives available to truckload shippers.)[5] Exit regulation created substantial excess capacity in rail

3. George J. Stigler, "The Theory of Economic Regulation," *Bell Journal of Economics*, vol. 2 (Spring 1971), pp. 3–21.

4. Clifford Winston, "Conceptual Developments in the Economics of Transportation: An Interpretive Survey," *Journal of Economic Literature*, vol. 23 (March 1985), p. 83.

5. John W. Snow, "The Problem of Motor Carrier Regulation and the Ford Administration's Proposal for Reform," in Paul W. MacAvoy and John W. Snow, eds., *Regulation of Entry and Pricing in Truck Transportation* (Washington: American Enterprise Institute, 1977), p. 5.

that amounted to annual production cost inefficiencies of roughly $2.5 billion.[6]

A third set of distortions, not precisely quantified, involves X-inefficiency costs amounting to several billion dollars. Two regulatory restrictions on the trucking industry substantially increased its operating costs. The first restriction prevented private trucking from acquiring return loads (backhauls) consisting of other firms' freight. The second designated the routes of regular route common carriers. And in both the trucking and rail industry, regulation stymied productivity growth, technological change, and management quality, again raising the cost of providing freight transportation service.[7] Saddled with regulation and inflated labor costs, the railroads' financial situation darkened to such an extent that by the mid-1970s a large fraction of rail service was not profitable.[8] Regulated motor carriers, especially in the less-than-truckload sector, and their labor force were still able to earn economic rents in the form of excess profits and wages, despite operating inefficiencies.[9] Finally, regulation had adverse effects on shippers, not only distorting their mode choices, but also limiting their ability to coordinate their location and inventory decisions with carriers.

Deregulation Legislation and Changes in Carrier Operations

The Staggers Rail Act of 1980 and the 1980 Motor Carrier Act did not completely deregulate the surface freight transportation industry, but they took significant steps in that direction.[10] The Staggers Act added considerable force to regulatory reforms enacted in the Railroad Revitalization and Regulatory Reform Act of 1976. Beginning in 1980, railroads were free to set their own rates without any ICC involvement for many com-

6. Winston, "Conceptual Developments," p. 84. For the most part this excess capacity resulted from too much trackage that was not warranted by traffic volume, not from too many parallel lines.
    7. Winston, "Conceptual Developments," p. 84.
    8. Theodore E. Keeler, *Railroads, Freight, and Public Policy* (Brookings, 1983), chap. 2.
    9. Thomas Gale Moore, "The Beneficiaries of Trucking Regulation," *Journal of Law and Economics*, vol. 21 (October 1978), pp. 327–43.
    10. For complete descriptions of the legislation, see Keeler, *Railroads, Freight, and Public Policy*; and Charles A. Taff, *Commercial Motor Transportation* (Cornell Maritime Press, 1986).

modities. The ICC exempted a number of commodities entirely and exempted movements where rates were set under contract. For other movements, railroad rates were subject to ICC market dominance and rate reasonableness guidelines. Market dominance was defined as having a ratio of revenues to variable costs for a given movement exceeding a specific level—1.6 in 1980, rising thereafter. A rate cannot be challenged today if the ratio of revenues to variable costs on the movement is less than 1.8. A rate exceeding this figure can be challenged successfully if two conditions exist. First, the railroad setting the rate must have no effective competition. Second, the rate has to be unreasonable; a rate for a coal shipment, for example, would be judged unreasonable if it were above stand-alone-cost, defined as the cost to any shipper (or shipper group) of serving it alone, as if it were isolated from the railroads' other customers. Final guidelines for rates for commodities other than coal have not yet been issued. The effect of the new maximum rate guidelines has been to give the railroads considerably more rate freedom.

The Staggers Act also set a rate minimum at variable costs. It allowed contract rates for all commodities, but it did not permit railroads to collude on rates through rate bureaus. It did allow railroads that cooperated in joint-line movements to work together to set joint-line rates, but restricted rate setting to those carriers participating in the movement.

The Staggers Act extended the 1976 legislation and ICC administrative actions by making it easier to abandon routes and to merge with other carriers. It required the ICC to complete the abandonment decision process within 255 days, and gave railroads latitude to justify abandonments on economic grounds. The act also required the ICC to make an initial decision on a merger application within 300 days, a step seen as encouraging the industry to pursue consolidations.

The Motor Carrier Act sought to increase industry competition, particularly in the less-than-truckload sector. Virtually all LTL shipments were moving under the collective rate bureau system, which, by stifling any member's attempt to file rates independently, effectively prevented price competition.[11] The legislation made it much easier for motor carriers to set rates independently by preventing rate bureaus from filing protests to the ICC against such rates. Collective ratemaking was prohibited for single-line rates and preserved only for joint-line rates and general rate increases. Entry into the industry was also much easier. The burden of

11. Snow, "Motor Carrier Regulation," p. 7.

proof in an entry application was no longer on the applicant, but on existing carriers, who could block entry only if they could show that it would be inconsistent with public convenience and necessity. Restrictions on private and contract carriers were reduced, enabling them to compete more directly with common carriers.

Rail and motor carrier operations changed dramatically in response to the movement toward deregulation. Railroads and shippers negotiated thousands of contract rates for regulated and unregulated commodities. The Association of American Railroads estimates that more than half of all rail traffic is currently shipped under some form of contract rate. Railroads also responded to their rate freedom by aggressively cutting rates in some markets and raising them in others. Facing far less opposition from the ICC, railroads abandoned thousands of miles of track, selling some of it to smaller regional and local or "short-line" railroads. In 1979 Class I railroads owned 277,242 miles of track; by 1987 this figure had fallen to 220,518.[12] Railroads also responded to more liberal merger policies. The Chessie (CSX), Norfolk-Southern, Union Pacific, and Burlington Northern consolidations were consummated in the early 1980s. Consolidation and abandonment reduced excess capacity and improved yard and linehaul operations, enabling railroads to lower their costs and offer substantially faster service.[13] Bankruptcy and consolidation, however, mean fewer major railroads. By 1988 sixteen Class I railroads, down from seventy-three in 1975, operated 82 percent of the system mileage and employed 90 percent of the industry labor force.[14]

Industry figures suggest that a huge influx of entry followed the Motor Carrier Act. In 1980, 18,045 motor carriers held ICC operating authority.

12. Association of American Railroads, *Railroad Facts, 1988* (Washington, November 1988). Not all of the reduction in Class I mileage resulted in elimination of rail service. According to a statement by Heather Gradison, Chairman ICC, before the Committee on Science, Commerce and Transportation, October 20, 1987, there were approximately 14,000 miles of short-line and regional railroads as of 1987, most of which were created after the Staggers Act.

13. These consolidations were primarily end-to-end, a type of rail merger that has been found to improve both service time and service time reliability substantially. See Robert G. Harris and Clifford Winston, "Potential Benefits of Rail Mergers: An Econometric Analysis of Network Effects on Service Quality," *Review of Economics and Statistics*, vol. 65 (February 1983), pp. 32–40.

14. AAR, *Railroad Facts, 1988*. Class I railroads were defined by the ICC as having at least $87.9 million in operating revenues in 1987. The threshold adjusts annually, but is not responsible for the decline in Class I carriers.

By 1986 that figure had more than doubled to 36,948.[15] The large surge in operating authority came primarily from small Class III carriers, which almost exclusively provide truckload service. These carriers increased from 14,610 in 1980 to 33,903 in 1986. The main source of this increase is from private carriers that took advantage of their ability to obtain backhaul authority given to them by the ICC in the Toto decision.[16] Other sources are owner-operators, who previously leased their service to common carriers, and carriers that operated in intrastate or exempt markets. Because most of these carriers operated in some truckload capacity during regulation, it is misleading to interpret industry figures as implying that motor carrier deregulation spawned thousands of new firms that entered the truckload sector.

Bankruptcies, mergers, and acquisitions cut the number of larger Class II motor carriers from 2,164 in 1980 to 1,387 in 1986.[17] New entry into less-than-truckload markets came largely from geographic expansion by existing carriers. Carriers have also been increasing the separation of truckload and less-than-truckload activities. Before deregulation, LTL general freight carriers derived roughly a third of their revenues from truckload traffic; by 1987 this figure had fallen to 12 percent.[18] LTL carriers took advantage of relaxed restrictions on entry by improving the efficiency of their networks.[19] In particular, carriers were able to reduce circuitry and empty backhauls. But because of the tremendous surge in competition, they also had to make greater promotional efforts and offer better service to acquire and keep business.

A big change in the truckload sector has been the growth of advanced truckload firms.[20] These firms offer premium service at such low cost that railroads face even more motor carrier competition, and some private trucking operations have been displaced. The salient aspect of advanced truckload operations is the explicit rejection of single-driver owner-operators (the mainstay of traditional TL operations) in favor of nonunion

---

15. "Trends and Statistics," *Commercial Carrier Journal*, July 1987, p. 100.

16. *Toto Purchasing and Supply Co., Inc.* 128 MCC 873 (March 24, 1978).

17. "Trends and Statistics," *Commercial Carrier Journal*, July 1987, p. 100.

18. Alex Brown & Sons, Inc., Research, "Wrap-up of the October 29 Trucking Seminar," Baltimore, Maryland, December 1987, p. 3.

19. LTL carriers parallel airlines in their use of hub-and-spoke networks. As in the case of airlines, deregulation's relaxation of entry restrictions facilitated efforts to optimize these networks.

20. See L. Lee Lane, "Innovation in Trucking: Advanced Truckload Firms," *Transportation Research Record*, no. 1154 (Washington: Transportation Research Board, 1987).

driver teams and relays, which keep tractors operating more hours each day. Advanced TL firms concentrate on high-density traffic corridors with balanced freight flows, thereby ensuring high vehicle use and low costs.[21]

Because deregulation and previous ICC actions eased backhaul and routing restrictions for private carriers, their operating costs also fell. Finally, intermodal (rail-motor carrier) operations increased initially with ICC implementation of Staggers Act provisions enabling railroads to expand operations with and to purchase motor carriers. However, the ICC's authority to approve railroad purchases of motor carriers was recently rescinded by the federal courts.[22]

From the shippers' perspective, the improvements in rail and motor carrier service were doubly attractive because they coincided with their efforts to cut down on inventory costs. One tool has been the change to just-in-time production and inventory management, which attempts to keep inventories to a minimum by bringing in raw materials and components just in time for production. Deregulation aided the development of this policy because shippers were freer to enter into contracts and to specify service standards that carriers had greater incentives and abilities to meet.

Summary

Deregulation appears to have changed both carrier and shipper behavior as policymakers intended. Carriers have taken significant steps to improve the efficiency of their operations and to set rates that are more responsive to competitive market conditions. Shippers have begun to coordinate their production activity more effectively with their transportation services. The economic effects of these responses will be evaluated in the next two chapters.

An industrial capital structure created and shaped for decades by regulation cannot be transformed overnight into a deregulated capital structure. A tremendous amount of excess capacity still remains to be squeezed from rail operations, including labor, track, yards, and terminals. And technical advances in equipment and in routing and scheduling proce-

21. Thomas M. Corsi and Curtis M. Grimm, "Changes in Owner-Operator Use, 1977–1985: Implications for Management Strategy," *Transportation Journal*, vol. 26 (Spring 1987), pp. 4–16.

22. *Regular Common Carrier Conference* v. *U.S.*, 820 F.2d 1323 (D.C. Cir. 1987).

dures—advances that have the potential to lower greatly the cost of railroad and motor carrier operations—are just beginning to be implemented on a wide scale. But the change has begun in earnest, and it is instructive to examine how carriers and shippers have been affected by deregulation as they just begin to shed more than one hundred years of regulation from their business practice.

Chapter Three

The Efficiency and Distributional Effects of Surface Freight Deregulation

THE EFFECTS of surface freight deregulation on society as a whole can best be evaluated by estimating separately how it has affected the economic welfare of shippers, carriers, and labor. The evaluation, however, presents a problem. With only a few minor exceptions, regulation and deregulation have not occurred simultaneously.[1] Simply comparing the economic welfare of the three affected groups before and after deregulation does not take into account the effects of contemporaneous changes in other economic factors, such as fuel prices and the business cycle, that will also affect shippers', carriers', and labor's welfare. Such changes should be isolated from the analysis because they occurred independently of the change in regulatory policy. At the same time, it is important to incorporate into the analysis all characteristics of the freight transportation environment that have changed because of deregulation.

Economists have long used a counterfactual approach to evaluate policy changes whose effects are confounded by the problems identified above.[2] As its name suggests, the counterfactual approach measures the effect of the initial policy on affected groups' economic welfare during a particular time and compares it with the effect that the alternative policy *would have had* on their welfare during the same time. Here, the counterfactual approach uses shipper, carrier, and labor behavior during 1985 to predict what their economic welfare would have been had deregulation occurred in 1977. We then compare that hypothetical welfare with their actual

---

1. A few commodities, such as motor carrier movements of produce, were exempted from regulation during the regulatory era. Proponents of deregulation used analysis of rates for these movements to argue that motor carrier deregulation of all commodities would lower rates. See Thomas Gale Moore, "Deregulating Surface Freight Transportation," in Almarin Phillips, ed., *Promoting Competition in Regulated Markets* (Brookings, 1975), pp. 55–98.

2. See Steven Morrison and Clifford Winston, *The Economic Effects of Airline Deregulation* (Brookings, 1986).

welfare under regulation during 1977.[3] Because the national economy was in a similar stage of the business cycle during both years, our findings should not be biased by cyclical effects.[4]

Effects on Shippers

The effects of deregulation on shippers are reflected in the value that shippers place on the change in rates and service quality offered by railroads, motor common carriers, and private trucking that is attributable to the change in regulatory policy. We measure this valuation by calculating shippers' compensating variations (CVs), the amount of money shippers could sacrifice following beneficial rate and service quality changes and be as well off after the changes as they were before them.

To perform this calculation we use a model, developed previously by Winston, to describe how shippers' decisions are influenced by rates and service quality of the different modes.[5] The model assumes that because freight service is subject to uncertainty, which is captured in the standard deviation and coefficient of variation in service time, shippers' mode choices are based on expected utility-maximizing behavior.[6] Their choices reflect discrete decisions for which probabilities of choice are estimated. The specification of the probability of choosing freight mode i ($Prob_i$),

3. It is also possible to use shipper, carrier, and labor behavior in 1977 to predict what the welfare of each group would be in 1985 had regulation still been in effect and to compare that welfare with their actual welfare in 1985. We do not take this approach because our demand model, which is the basis for evaluating the benefits to shippers, was estimated from 1977 data, and unnecessary imprecision would be introduced by using the coefficients to predict the effects of deregulation on shippers' welfare for 1985. On the other hand, the coefficients are not likely to be influenced by the change in regulatory regime. Thus, use of a demand model estimated during regulation is not inappropriate, and the choice of which counterfactual approach to take should not affect conclusions.

4. We selected 1985 as our deregulated period for this reason. Both economies were in a stage of economic expansion, with unemployment slightly lower and corporate profits as a share of GNP slightly higher in 1977 than in 1985. Another possible source of bias, secular growth in freight transportation, should be small because of the maturity of the industries and the virtual absence of cyclical effects.

5. Clifford Winston, "A Disaggregate Model of the Demand for Intercity Freight Transportation," *Econometrica*, vol. 49 (July 1981), pp. 981–1006.

6. The coefficient of variation is the ratio of the standard deviation to the mean. The coefficient of variation and the standard deviation measure the reliability of service time. An alternative measure, which poses greater data difficulties, is the probability of a shipment meeting a certain service standard, for example, three days.

where rail, private trucking, and motor common carrier are the possible alternatives, is given by

Prob$_i$ = f(Freight charges$_j$, Average transit time$_j$, Standard deviation of transit time$_j$, Coefficient of variation of transit time$_j$, Shipment size, Value of commodity shipped, Distance of shipping firm from a rail siding, Sales of shipping firm, j = 1, 2, 3).[7]

The model was estimated from a sample of shipments during 1977 that included all major commodity groups except coal and grain.[8]

The value that shippers place on freight charges and service time variables can be seen from the elasticities and values of time based on parameter estimates of this model (table 3-1). As the table shows, the influence of rates and service time on shippers' decisions about whether to use rail, motor common carrier, or private truck depends on the commodity shipped.

---

7. The formal specification of the choice probability for the ith mode, *Prob$_i$*, which is given by a trinomial probit model is

$$Prob_i = \int_{r_j = -\infty}^{V_i - V_j} \int_{r_k = -\infty}^{V_i - V_k} n\ (r;\ O,\ \Omega)\ dr_j\ dr_k\ ,$$

where $n(r;O,\Omega)$ is the multivariate normal frequency function with mean vector O and covariance matrix Ω evaluated at argument r. The mean expected utility of a mode, V, is a linear parametric function of the explanatory variables given in the text.

8. Coal and grain commodities could not be included in the estimation of a mode choice model because of the unavailability of data on truck movements of these commodities. Because our sample is choice-based—that is, a random sample of shipments was collected from each mode—sampling weights had to be used during estimation to ensure that aggregate mode shares in the sample were consistent with aggregate mode shares in the population. The sampling weights were also used for all calculations carried out with the model. Produce shipments and their motor carrier and rail freight charges and service times are from the Federal Railroad Administration, *A Long-Term Study of Produce Transportation,* Report No. FRA-OOPD-78-2.9 (U.S. Department of Transportation, December 1977). The rail shipments for the other commodity groups were based on a sample begun with the U.S. Interstate Commerce Commission, "Rail Freight Adequacy Study," *Ex Parte* no. 270 (1973); the private trucking shipments are from Bureau of Economics, "Empty/ Loaded Truck Miles on Interstate Highways during 1976" (Interstate Commerce Commission, April 1977); the motor common carrier shipments are from various traffic consulting firms. The 1977 rail and motor carrier freight charges were determined from ICC rate books. Private truck costs are based on unpublished data from the Association of American Railroads' Private Truck and Driver Cost Model, Washington, May 1978. The rail service times are from the Association of American Railroads Train II data base; the motor carrier service times were provided by Roadway and Yellow Freight Systems; and the private trucking service times are based on unpublished data from the U.S. Interstate Commerce Commission Intercity Driving Time Report for 1977. The final sample sizes were 863 produce shipments and 1,210 shipments of the other commodities.

Table 3-1. *Selected Estimates Derived from Intercity Freight Demand Model*

	Elasticity	
Variable	*Maximum*	*Minimum*
Rail rate	Transport equipment −2.68	Lumber −0.08
Motor common carrier rate	Leather, rubber, plastic products −2.97	Machinery −0.04
Private truck cost	Transport equipment −2.96	Lumber −0.14
Rail service time	Fresh produce −2.33	Paper products −0.07
Motor common carrier service time	Agricultural products −0.59	Chemicals −0.46
Private truck service time	Fresh produce −0.69	Paper products −0.15

Source: Clifford Winston, "A Disaggregate Model of the Demand for Intercity Freight Transportation," *Econometrica*, vol. 49 (July 1981), pp. 981–1006.

The influence of freight charges, as reflected by their elasticities, can be substantial or negligible. For example, a 10 percent decline in rail rates for transport equipment would lead to a 26.8 percent increase in the probability of selecting rail for these shipments, but the same decline in rail rates for lumber would lead to only a 0.8 percent increase in the probability of selecting rail. Similar effects also exist for service time.

A clearer picture of the importance of service attributes emerges if one thinks of the value shippers place on shortening service time as an implicit discount rate. For some commodities, this discount rate is consistent with historical real rates of return, and for other commodities it is substantially higher. In the case of rail, for example, shippers of fresh produce value transit time as high as 21 percent of the shipment value itself, while shippers of primary and fabricated metals value transit time at 6 percent of the shipment value. In the case of private trucks, fresh produce shippers' value of transit time is 18 percent of the shipment value, while primary and fabricated metals shippers' value is 8 percent.

What explains the different valuations? The costs associated with mean transit time are the interest and storage costs of holding inventories, obsolescence costs, and in-transit interest costs. Shippers who use modes with slower transit times need larger inventories to meet unexpected demand and to avoid stockout costs. Obsolescence costs are associated with slow transit times that drastically lower the value of shipments such as newspapers and fresh produce. In-transit interest costs are self-explanatory. A high discount rate could reflect one or all of these components.

Small farmers shipping produce may have very high implicit discount rates simply because the obsolescence (spoilage) costs associated with slow transit time could put them out of business.

Shippers' value of the reliability of transit time is also motivated by inventory and obsolescence cost considerations. Inventory costs arise from unreliable service because of stockouts that may occur regardless of the randomness in demand. Obsolescence costs could arise from a large positive deviation from average transit time. The value of improvements in the average speed of service and reliability caused by deregulation therefore reflect real reductions in firms' production costs.

Our demand model treats several variables that are likely to be influenced by deregulation as if they were not. Shippers, for example, will almost certainly adjust their shipment sizes, shipment frequencies, and possibly their locations to avoid rate increases, to take advantage of a general reduction in rates or changes in rate schedules that reward larger shipping volumes, and to lower inventory costs. They could also change shipment sizes, frequencies, and location in response to service improvements and new technological opportunities.[9] Because our demand model does not take into account the possibility of shippers' making these adjustments, our analysis will understate the benefits to shippers due to deregulation.[10]

Compensating Variations

For the sample of commodity groups estimated by our demand model, we can calculate compensating variations (CVs), a measure of the benefits

9. For example, technological innovations such as double stack container trains have spurred the growth in container traffic.

10. Changes over time in the mix of commodities carried by modes because of traffic shifts and changes in commodity markets unrelated to deregulation could also introduce bias. According to the Association of American Railroads, the shares of commodities for which rail and truck primarily compete were virtually unchanged from 1977 to 1985. See Association of American Railroads, *Railroad Facts* (Washington, 1978 and 1986). But rail has increased its share of coal and grain tonnage and decreased its share of miscellaneous commodities tonnage, a change that is accounted for in our analysis of rail profitability. By using economies in a similar stage in the business cycle, we control for differences in most commodity markets. However, rail rates have most likely been affected by real declines in coal and grain prices during 1977–85, declines that are unrelated to deregulation. The effects on rail rates of these declining prices will partially offset the conservative approach toward estimating rate changes noted above.

of deregulation to shippers that converts into an equivalent dollar value the changes in the prices and transit times of the different freight modes and the probability of selecting a mode.[11] Because the change in shippers' welfare comes from simultaneous price and service quality changes in rail, motor common carrier, and private trucking, a shipper can benefit from improvements in the mode preferred both before and after deregulation or he can benefit by switching to a mode that has become the preferred alternative under deregulation.[12]

Coal and grain shippers will be affected primarily by changes in railroad rates due to deregulation. Although we were unable to include coal and grain commodities in the estimation of a mode choice model, we can calculate the change in shippers' benefits (surplus) caused by rail rate deregulation. The expression, given as a percentage of rail revenues is

11. Formally the CV is given by the following expression:

$$CV = -\frac{1}{\lambda} \int_{V^o}^{V^f} \sum_{i=1}^{3} Prob_i \, (V) \, dV,$$

where V^o and V^f represent shippers' expected utility under regulation (o) and deregulation (f), respectively, $Prob_i$ represents the probability of selecting freight mode i, and λ converts the expression into a dollar value. Based on Roy's Identity, λ is the coefficient of freight charges. The integral in this expression can be interpreted as the expected value of the maximum utility of the freight mode alternatives. Thus, by multiplying the change in the expected value of maximum utility (measured in "utils"), by the conversion factor λ (measured in dollars per util), we obtain the compensating variation, the amount of money shippers could sacrifice following deregulation and be as well off as they were before deregulation.

12. Because we are calculating the change in shippers' welfare from simultaneous price and service quality changes in rail (r), motor common carrier (t), and private trucking (p), it is necessary to specify a valid path for the line integral given in the preceding footnote. Thus,

$$CV = -\frac{1}{\lambda} \left[\int_{V_r^o}^{V_r^f} Prob_r \, (V_r, \, V_t^o, \, V_p^o) \, dV_r \right.$$
$$+ \int_{V_t^o}^{V_t^f} Prob_t \, (V_r^f, \, V_t, \, V_p^o) \, dV_t$$
$$\left. + \int_{V_p^o}^{V_p^f} Prob_p \, (V_r^f, \, V_t^f, \, V_p) \, dV_p \right].$$

Calculation of this expression yields a CV per shipment attributable to surface freight deregulation. Sample enumeration is used to obtain a weighted average CV as a fraction of shipment value for each commodity group in the sample. Aggregate results are obtained by multiplying these figures by the total value of each commodity group based on the 1977 U.S. Census of Transportation. Our findings are independent of the path of integration because the demand model satisfies the cross-price symmetry conditions.

$$\frac{Surplus\ change}{revenues} = \frac{1}{2} t^2 \epsilon + t,$$

where t is the percentage change in railroad rates and ϵ the price elasticity of rail demand, which we set to -0.33.[13]

Sample

The change in shippers' welfare due to deregulation is calculated using a sample of shipments made during 1977. All major commodity groups are included in the sample.[14] On the basis of 1985 shipping activity, deregulated freight charges and service times for our sample of shipments had to be obtained and converted into 1977 counterfactual deregulated values. Because of the complexity involved in determining deregulated rates and service times, we construct a base case and then perform sensitivity analysis.

Motor Carrier Rates

Deregulated (1985) motor carrier rates for our shipments are those of a representative truckload carrier and a representative less-than-truckload carrier. The reasonableness of these rates was corroborated by rates from

13. This second-order approximation was used in Zvi Griliches, "Research Costs and Social Returns: Hybrid Corn and Related Innovations," *Journal of Political Economy*, vol. 66 (October 1958), pp. 419-31. We use the derived demand formula $\epsilon = k\epsilon_d$ where k is the share of rail transport costs of coal as a fraction of the total production costs of coal and ϵ_d is the demand elasticity of coal, to determine the price elasticity of rail transport of coal. Based on figures presented in Martin B. Zimmerman, *The U.S. Coal Industry: The Economics of Policy Choice* (MIT Press, 1981), the rail demand elasticity is -0.33. We assume the same value for grain. This assumption is partly corroborated by Andrew F. Daughety and Fred S. Inaba, "Empirical Aspects of Service-Differentiated Transport Demand," Proceedings of the Workshop on Motor Carrier Economic Regulation, National Academy of Sciences, 1978, pp. 329–49, who find that multiple-rail car grain shippers' own and cross elasticities are generally small. Our results for coal and grain were not particularly sensitive to the assumed elasticity. The 677 coal and 1,042 grain shipments that form the basis of this calculation and their regulated rail freight charges are from the 1977 ICC Waybill Tapes. The 1977 shipments were matched with 1985 shipments using the first four digits (roughly the county level) of the standard point location code. Aggregate results were obtained by multiplying the weighted average (surplus change ÷ revenue) for coal and grain by the total rail revenues for coal and grain obtained from the Waybill Tapes.

14. The data sources for the shipments were given in footnotes 8 and 13.

a transcontinental carrier providing LTL and TL service. A representative range of percentage discounts was provided along with the LTL rates. For the base case we used the average LTL discount of 25 percent. Truckload rates were given as zip-code (point-to-point) rates.

We cannot use a standard truck rate deflator to predict what the 1985 rates would have been in a 1977 deregulated environment because standard deflators include the effect of the change in regulatory policy. We therefore construct our own TL and LTL counterfactual rate deflators to deflate 1985 rates to 1977 deregulated rates. The procedure is to estimate reduced-form linear regressions that relate average rate (revenues divided by tons) to input prices (price of fuel, average compensation, and insurance expense) and output characteristics (average length of haul, average load size, and, for LTL rates, average shipment size and the share of revenues derived from LTL operations).[15] We then insert 1985 mean values of the explanatory variables to predict the average 1985 rate, and deflate the factor prices to 1977 and assume that output characteristics are unchanged to predict the average 1977 deregulated rate. In the process of deflating the factor prices we adjust the LTL wage deflator to account for deregulation's effect on wages in this sector.[16] The deflators are the ratios of the predicted average rates for 1985 and 1977.[17]

The estimated parameters for the rate regressions, which have the correct signs and plausible magnitudes, are presented in table 3-2.[18] The deflators are

15. LTL carriers typically carry LTL and TL shipments. Because LTL shipments generally require sorting at a terminal, they are more costly to ship. The rate regressions are estimated from carrier data for 1984–85. All variables are from the ICC Annual Reports as compiled in the American Trucking Association data tapes. Attempts were made to include the price of capital, but this effect was small and statistically insignificant.

16. Specific deflators are used to deflate the factor prices to 1977. Following Nancy Rose, "Labor Rent Sharing and Regulation: Evidence from the Trucking Industry," *Journal of Political Economy*, vol. 95 (December 1987), pp. 1146–78, we increase the wage deflator for LTL carriers by 20 percent. We could find no evidence that wages in the more competitive TL sector were inflated by regulation.

17. This procedure and a similar one used in our analysis of the effects of deregulation on carrier profitability implicitly assume that the underlying technological relations existing during 1985 also existed in the 1977 deregulated environment. One cannot appeal to noncounterfactual evidence pertaining to the 1977 regulated environment and the 1985 deregulated environment to evaluate this assumption.

18. Although the coefficients for fuel price and average compensation are considerably different for TL and LTL carriers, the elasticities for these variables are similar. The TL fuel price elasticity is 0.11; the LTL fuel price elasticity, 0.20. The TL compensation elasticity is 0.25; the LTL compensation elasticity, 0.53. The somewhat higher compen-

Table 3-2. *Truckload and Less-Than-Truckload Rate Regressions*

	Coefficient	
Variable	*Truckload*[a]	*Less-than-truckload*[b]
Constant	17.5222	−28.8057
	(5.5366)	(10.1245)
Fuel price (dollars per gallon)	1.0439	7.5965
	(2.9023)	(4.8127)
Average compensation	0.2459	1.6142
(thousands of dollars per year)	(0.1267)	(0.2093)
Insurance expenditures	16.1945	18.6840
(dollars per ton)	(0.5566)	(0.7713)
Average length of haul (miles)	0.0300	0.0539
	(0.0024)	(0.0071)
Average load (tons)	−1.2345	−0.9980
	(0.1387)	(0.4092)
Average shipment size (tons)	. . .	−1.0675
		(0.3283)
LTL revenue as a percentage of total	. . .	0.2530
revenue		(0.0694)

Source: Authors' calculations.
a. $R^2 = 0.75$; number of observations $= 737$. Standard errors are in parentheses.
b. $R^2 = 0.83$; number of observations $= 350$. Standard errors are in parentheses.

$$TL\ deflator\ =\ \frac{Predicted\ average\ rate\ (1985)}{Predicted\ average\ rate\ (1977)}\ =\ 1.55$$

$$LTL\ deflator\ =\ \frac{Predicted\ average\ rate\ (1985)}{Predicted\ average\ rate\ (1977)}\ =\ 2.16.$$

We deflate 1985 TL and LTL rates by these figures to obtain 1977 deregulated rates.

The plausibility of these deflators can be established by comparing them with alternative deflators. A TL rate deflator based on actual rate changes during 1977–85 is 1.51. Our deflator therefore suggests that deregulation has slightly lowered TL rates, a plausible conclusion for a sector of the trucking industry that was highly competitive before deregulation. An LTL deflator based on actual rate changes during 1977–85

---

sation elasticity for LTL carriers arises from the larger share of labor costs in their total costs.

is 1.79.[19] Our deflator therefore implies that deregulation has substantially lowered rates in this sector, again a plausible conclusion because regulation severely impeded competition among LTL carriers.

Private Truck Costs

Deregulation has lowered private trucking costs by making it easier for these operations to secure loads as for-hire carriers, which reduces the mileage they travel empty. Estimates by the Association of American Railroads reveal that the costs of private trucking would be as much as 35 percent higher under regulation than they are under deregulation.[20] Thus, as a conservative base case estimate, we reduce private trucking costs (freight charges) under regulation 20 percent to get deregulated private trucking costs.

Railroad Freight Rates

Deregulation has significantly changed the way railroads set freight rates. As a simplification, railroad shipments now move at contract rates, at discounts from the tariff rate, or at tariff rates. The deregulated railroad charges we use for all commodities except coal and grain came directly from the railroads.[21] We asked them to supply us with a representative 1985 contract rate, discounted tariff rate, and tariff rate for each of our shipments that they could carry. We therefore had rates from more than one railroad for many shipments. Within each classification, the rates

19. Both TL and LTL deflators are from Eno Foundation for Transportation, Inc., *Transportation in America, A Statistical Analysis of Transportation in the U.S.*, 7th ed. (Westport, Conn., May 1989), p. 12.

20. Unpublished report from Association of American Railroads, Intermodal Policy Division, June 1987.

21. We asked railroads directly for their rates because published rates for unregulated commodities are highly suspect. The railroads that kindly supplied deregulated rates for this study are CSX, Burlington Northern, Southern Pacific, Union Pacific, Santa Fe, Illinois Central Gulf, Conrail, and Norfolk-Southern. The deregulated charges for coal and grain shipments, which are regulated commodities, are from the 1985 ICC Waybill Tape. It has been alleged that these charges are suspect because they do not include end-of-year adjustments in contract charges, which arise if a shipper exceeds or falls short of the agreed-upon annual shipping volume. We investigated the possible bias by comparing the total revenues in 1985 derived from coal and grain shipments as predicted by the Waybill data with the total 1985 revenues from coal and grain shipments presented in American Association of Railroads, *Railroad Facts, 1986,* and found only a small difference.

were broadly consistent across carriers. For the base case we used the average contract or discounted tariff rate when one was available; otherwise, we used the tariff rate. A breakdown of the structure of rates for the sample was consistent with the population structure: more than half of our shipments move at a contract rate.

Because rail rate deregulation was expected to have different effects for different commodities, we attempted to construct counterfactual rail rate deflators by commodity group.[22] Stymied by data limitations, we constructed, instead, rail rate deflators for individual commodity groups based on actual rate changes during 1977-85.[23] By drawing on Henry McFarland's efforts to reconcile the findings of previous studies that used a dummy variable to measure the effect of deregulation on rail rates, we then decided how, if at all, these deflators should be adjusted to become counterfactual deflators.[24] McFarland's conclusion that rail deregulation had a statistically insignificant effect on rates convinced us to use the actual deflators as counterfactual deflators.[25] The deflators, which are displayed in table 3-3, cluster around 1.89 but reveal some variation that is useful to capture. Each rate was adjusted by the appropriate rail rate deflator to obtain the 1977 counterfactual deregulated rate.[26]

Service Quality

The dimensions of service quality that we include are average transit time, the standard deviation of transit time, and the coefficient of variation

22. Recall that Boyer found that regulated railroad rates had a much stronger value-of-service component than motor carrier rates. See Boyer, "Equalizing Discrimination."

23. These deflators are from the Bureau of Labor Statistics, Division of Industrial Prices and Price Indexes (Railroads, linehaul operations). They are constructed from actual transaction prices, but they are conservative because, like our study, they hold shipment size and commodity characteristics constant. The assumption of constant shipment size is especially likely to make the grain rate deflators conservative because grain shipments receive large discounts by moving at much larger volumes on unit trains. This conservative bias, however, is partially offset because the larger shipment sizes impose higher costs on shippers who must invest in improved handling facilities and because of declines in the real price of grain unrelated to deregulation that could affect rail grain rates.

24. Henry McFarland, "The Effects of United States Railroad Deregulation on Shippers, Labor, and Capital," *Journal of Regulatory Economics,* vol. 1 (1989), pp. 259–70.

25. Ideally, the effect of the deregulation dummy would vary by commodity group and rate classification (contract, tariff, discounted tariff). Unfortunately, this variation could not be captured. The sensitivity of our findings to alternative assumptions regarding the rate deflators and rate classifications is explored later.

26. In the case of coal and grain shipments, the 1985 freight charges are adjusted by the rate deflators to obtain 1977 counterfactual deregulated charges, which are used to construct the percentage change in rates, t, in the surplus change formula.

Table 3-3. *Railroad Rate Deflators*

Commodity	Deflator
Coal	1.90
Grain	1.90
Fresh produce	1.89
Agricultural products	1.92
Wood, lumber, and furniture	2.00
Chemicals	1.84
Petroleum, petroleum products	1.90
Stone, clay, and glass products	1.95
Primary and fabricated metals	1.77
Transportation equipment	1.69
Paper, printing, and publishing	1.86
Leather, rubber, and plastic products	1.89
Machinery including electrical machinery	1.89
Textiles and fabricated textiles	1.89
All commodities	1.89

Sources: Bureau of Labor Statistics and authors' calculations.

of transit time. The data sources for the service times during 1977 have been described previously (see footnote 8). The mean and standard deviation of deregulated (1985) railroad transit time for our shipments are based on measurements made from data provided by the Association of American Railroads. We tried to ensure that the car types and number of movements used to construct regulated rail service times for our sample were comparable to those used to construct deregulated service times. Using these samples, we found that rail's mean transit time had improved as a result of deregulation by nearly 30 percent and that its standard deviation had improved even more. Because these results were very sensitive to changes in the car types and the number of movements in the samples, we assumed base case deregulated service times by lowering the regulated service times for each of our shipments 20 percent.[27]

Motor carrier service times under deregulation are based on mean and standard deviation service standards set by representative TL and LTL

27. According to an internal memo, based on a car cycle analysis for boxcar movements, the Association of American Railroads Freight Equipment Management Program found that mean transit time fell roughly 21.5 percent from 1978 to 1986 when length of haul was held constant. A related AAR study of reliability, based on truck-on-flatcar (TOFC) movements, found even greater improvements for the same period.

motor carriers. The mean service standards are consistent with those presented by Robert Delaney.[28] Lacking external corroboration for the standard deviation, we include only changes in the mean transit time in the base case.

Deregulation is likely to be the chief cause of any change in service: shippers now view service standards as an important part of expanded negotiations (contracts) with carriers, and carriers have grown increasingly responsive to these concerns because of greater inter- and intramodal competition and changes they have made in their networks to improve service. In the case of rail, these improvements are largely attributable to end-to-end mergers that have been encouraged by the ICC under deregulation.

Three dimensions of service quality that we do *not* measure have also probably improved under deregulation. It has been argued that the time between a shipper's request for service and the arrival of a carrier at the dock has decreased under deregulation because carriers recognize its importance to shippers' use of just-in-time inventory management. Rail shippers are now also able to tailor their service through contracts; for example, they can specify certain types of equipment with the contract rate. Finally, more frequent rail and motor carrier service allows shippers to transport smaller shipments and to hold down inventory costs. We quantify none of these benefits.[29]

Findings

The effects of surface freight deregulation on shippers', and thus ultimately on final consumers', economic welfare are presented in table 3-4. Overall, shippers have reaped $11 billion (1977 dollars) in annual benefits ($20 billion when expressed in 1988 dollars).[30] All modes have contributed sizable net benefits.[31] Deregulation of trucking has had its expected effects: private trucking operating costs have fallen, generating

28. Robert V. Delaney, "The Disunited States: A Country in Search of an Efficient Transportation Policy," CATO Institute Policy Analysis, Washington, March 1987.
29. The effect of deregulation on shipment loss and damage is also not analyzed. The impact of this omission is not clear.
30. The estimate is inflated to 1988 dollars with a gross domestic product (GDP) inflator.
31. This is consistent with our forecasts of mode shares, which show little change as a result of the change in regulatory policy.

Table 3-4. *Base Case Shippers' Welfare Change between Regulation and Counterfactual Deregulation*[a]

Billions of 1977 dollars

Item	Effect
Private truck costs	3.03
Motor common carrier rates	3.96
Motor common carrier service time	0.82
Rail rates	
All commodities excluding coal and grain	− 1.33
Coal	− .02
Grain	0.28
Total	− 1.07
Rail service time	4.69
Total welfare change	10.97

Source: Authors' calculations.
a. The sum of the components is not equal to the total welfare change because the welfare measure (CV) is nonlinear.

$3 billion in benefits to shippers; the increased competition in the motor common carrier industry has caused rate reductions that amount to $4 billion in benefits, almost all of which are from the LTL sector, and service improvements that have produced nearly another billion dollars in benefits. The benefits from railroad deregulation have not come from rate reductions. Rail, never a premium service mode, has been able to generate benefits by making use of the considerable room it had for service improvement. Rail service time improvements and shippers' value of them have contributed nearly $5 billion of benefits. As expected, rail rate deregulation has resulted in a reshuffling of rates; rates have fallen for grain shipments, but risen for coal shipments.[32] Gains and losses for the other commodities have resulted in an overall loss to shippers of slightly more than $1 billion.[33]

32. These findings are consistent with other studies. Scott Atkinson and Joe Kerkvliet find coal rate increases, and James MacDonald finds grain rate decreases due to deregulation. See Scott E. Atkinson and Joe Kerkvliet, "Measuring the Multilateral Allocation of Rents: Wyoming Low-Sulfur Coal," *Rand Journal of Economics,* vol. 17 (Autumn 1986), pp. 416–30; and James M. MacDonald, "Railroad Deregulation, Innovation, and Competition: Effects of the Staggers Act on Grain Transportation," *Journal of Law and Economics,* vol. 32 (April 1989), pp. 63–95.

33. Confidentiality agreements prevent us from presenting results for individual commodity groups. Nonetheless, protests that have been filed at the ICC for sugar, electrical equipment, recyclables, and spent nuclear fuel are suggestive of which shippers were relatively disadvantaged by rate deregulation. As pointed out in Clifford Winston, "Con-

Given that the entire surface freight transportation system was deregulated, results pertaining to a specific mode should be interpreted with some caution because they do not explicitly capture that mode's impact on another mode's rates and service. For example, in our sample the average change in railroad rates due to deregulation shows a slight decline when the change is not weighted by the probability of rail being selected. When the probability of choosing rail, which reflects the change in motor carrier rates and in private trucking costs due to deregulation, is used to weight the average change in rail rates, the average change in rates goes up rather than down. Rail rates have frequently declined where trucks have cut their rates and are thus able to win the traffic. But certain rail rate cuts, even if they are not rewarded by increased traffic, have affected truck rates and have thus benefited shippers.

Corroborative Evidence and Sensitivity Analysis

Our conclusion that freight deregulation has strongly benefited shippers is consistent with other evidence.[34] But two of our specific findings require further explanation. Delaney claims that the annual inventory cost savings due to motor carrier deregulation amount to more than $50 billion, a finding that is an order of magnitude greater than our own.[35] But Delaney's estimate is not based on shippers' revealed preference of their value of service improvements, nor is it based on a counterfactual analysis that controls for factors besides deregulation that have affected inventory costs. Because macroeconomic growth and higher real interest rates during the

---

ceptual Developments in the Economics of Transportation: An Interpretive Survey," *Journal of Economic Literature,* vol. 23 (March 1985), p. 83, economists thought it was possible that rail rate deregulation could lead to a welfare loss to shippers in return for improvements in rail's financial viability. For detailed simulations that illustrate this trade-off, see Richard C. Levin, "Railroad Rates, Profitability, and Welfare under Deregulation," *Bell Journal of Economics,* vol. 12 (Spring 1981), pp. 1–26. Although the rail rate deflators suggest that deregulation had no effect on rates, in our model shippers could experience a net loss from rate deregulation because captive shippers had to absorb rate increases and noncaptive shippers shifted to truck even when rail rates fell, because truck rates fell more.

34. See Diane S. Owen, "Deregulation in the Trucking Industry," Federal Trade Commission, Bureau of Economics, May 1988; and Christopher C. Barnekov, "The Track Record," *Regulation,* no. 1 (1987), pp. 19–27.

35. Delaney, "The Disunited States."

1980s have greatly reduced inventories, Delaney's estimate, which attributes these effects to deregulation, is almost certainly inflated.[36]

A second source of controversy has been the effects of deregulation on rail rates. We found that deregulation led, on average, to higher rates, although we admittedly made restrictive assumptions regarding shippers' responses to rate changes. Our finding can be compared with the results from two aggregate estimates of the effects of rail rate deregulation.[37] The first estimate, by Kenneth Boyer, is a simple time-series model that isolates the effect of deregulation on rail rates.[38] Boyer found that the most likely effect of deregulation was to raise rail rates, a finding consistent with our own.[39]

But simply using aggregate data to calculate the 1977 counterfactual deregulated average rail revenue per ton, $12.86, and then comparing it with the actual 1977 average rail revenue per ton of $13.90 appears to contradict our finding.[40] Unlike our analysis, however, this calculation allows shipment size and length of haul to change during the change in

36. Valerie A. Ramey, "Inventories as Factors of Production and Economic Fluctuations," *American Economic Review,* vol. 79 (June 1989), pp. 338–54, finds inventories negatively related to real interest rates.

37. We are unaware of any disaggregate analyses of the effects of freight deregulation for a full range of commodity groups.

38. Kenneth D. Boyer, "The Costs of Price Regulation: Lessons from Railroad Deregulation," *Rand Journal of Economics,* vol. 18 (Autumn 1987), pp. 408–16. Like our analysis, Boyer's does not use post-1985 data. He partially controls for shipment size by including train weight in his specification, but unlike our study, his allows average length of haul to vary.

39. Boyer's estimate of the welfare loss to shippers is roughly $0.4 billion (1977 dollars). Our loss estimate is greater because unlike Boyer we hold the shipping network constant, and thus do not capture any rate reductions from the increase in the average length of haul due to deregulation (see below).

40. This comparison, which led to similar conclusions when revenue per ton mile was used instead of revenue per ton, draws on data from the Association of American Railroads, *Railroad Facts, 1986.* The 1985 average rail revenue per ton is $21.39. But this average is low because of rail's tendency to increase its share of lower-value (yield) commodities like coal. Rail's share of bulk commodities has risen 12 percentage points from 1977 to 1985. This increase is primarily attributable to changes in the macroeconomy that have increased the demand for coal. Christopher C. Barnekov and Andrew N. Kleit, "The Costs of Railroad Regulation: A Further Analysis," *International Journal of Transport Economics* (forthcoming), find that the elasticity of rail rates with respect to the percentage share of bulk commodities is roughly − 1.0. Thus, for our counterfactual comparison we increased the 1985 average rail revenue per ton by 13.6 percent to account for the 12 percent decline in rail rates that was attributable to commodity shifts. This figure was deflated by our counterfactual rail rate deflator, 1.89, to obtain the 1977 counterfactual average rate per ton.

regulatory regime. During 1977–85, shipment size increased 13 percent and average length of haul increased 15.6 percent.[41] Because most of this increase is attributable to deregulation, the preceeding calculation mainly illustrates the conservative, although internally consistent, nature of our finding. To show this, we simulate the effect of allowing shipment size and length of haul to increase in our analysis by increasing our rail rate deflators and find that shippers benefited from rail rate deregulation by $0.22 billion (1977 dollars).[42]

All our findings are based on rather conservative assumptions regarding carriers' rates and service times. We show the sensitivity of our findings to the primary assumptions in table 3-5. Under even more conservative assumptions than those of the base case, deregulation still yields $4.62 billion (1977 dollars) in benefits. All modes contribute benefits, but rail's contribution is small. Under more liberal assumptions, which are still within the range of plausibility, deregulation yields $16.54 billion (1977 dollars) in benefits, with every change in rates and service quality in every mode producing benefits. Thus, our qualitative conclusion is robust; a reliable conservative estimate of the annual benefits to shippers due to deregulation is some $11 billion (1977 dollars), while more and less conservative assumptions adjust the estimate down and up by roughly $6 billion.

Effects on Carriers

To estimate the effects of deregulation on motor carriers and railroads, we construct a counterfactual projection of what their economic profits would have been had deregulation been under way in 1977 and compare the projection with actual profits in 1977. To identify the effects of deregulation on carriers more precisely, we provide separate calculations of the change in revenues and costs.[43]

41. Association of American Railroads, *Railroad Facts, 1986*.
42. Using our railroad cost function (see below), we found that increasing shipment size 13 percent and length of haul 15.6 percent lowered railroad costs roughly 12 percent. Thus, we increased our rail rate deflators 13.6 percent to capture the decline in rail rates from lower costs. These adjustments are conservative because they do not account for any increase in intra- and intermodal competition that larger shipment sizes and longer lengths of haul might generate.
43. We estimate cost functions for motor carriers and railroads to predict the change in costs. Because the cost functions are used for prediction purposes it is important to focus

Table 3-5. *Sensitivity Analysis of Welfare Change between Regulation and Counterfactual Deregulation*[a]
Billions of 1977 dollars

Item	Base case assumption	Effect	Lower bound assumption	Effect	Upper bound assumption	Effect
Private truck costs	20 percent decline	3.03	10 percent decline	1.42	30 percent decline	4.95
Motor common carrier rates	25 percent LTL discount	3.96	10 percent LTL discount	2.57	35 percent LTL discount	4.90
Motor common carrier service time	Mean improves	0.82	No improvement	0.00	Mean and standard deviation improve	0.85
Rail rates	Average contract or discount tariff when available, tariff rate otherwise	−1.07	Average contract and tariff rate	−1.62	Lowest available rate	0.78
Rail service time[b]	20 percent improvement in mean and standard deviation	4.69	10 percent improvement in mean and standard deviation	2.29	25 percent improvement in mean and standard deviation	5.90
Total welfare change	. . .	10.97	. . .	4.62	. . .	16.54

Source: Authors' calculations.
a. The sum of the components is not equal to the total welfare change because the welfare measure (CV) is nonlinear.
b. Use of the change in service time based on our disaggregated service time data produced welfare improvements to shippers that were greater than our upper bound assumptions. As indicated previously, we are cautious about using these data at the disaggregate city-pair level because of their sensitivity to car types considered and relative sample sizes.

Motor Carriers

We estimated separate cost functions for truckload and less-than-truck-load motor carriers. Total costs for TL carriers are specified as a function of output (ton miles), output characteristics (average length of haul, average load), and factor prices (average compensation, fuel price, and insurance expenditures).[44] Because LTL carriers employ hub and spoke networks, using terminals as hubs, their specification also included route density, and we also included the share of LTL revenue in their total revenue.[45] We investigated various functional forms and obtained the most plausible results from a log-linear (Cobb-Douglas) specification estimated by least squares.[46] The estimated parameters, which have the correct signs

---

primarily on the plausibility of our predictions rather than on the accuracy of particular coefficients. As in other transportation cost estimation, we treat output as exogenous. This assumption is probably still reasonable for motor carriers under deregulation, but questionable for railroads. The standard way to control or test for output endogeneity is to use instrumental variables, but we were unable to specify a satisfactory set of instruments. Nonetheless, as we show below, our predictions of total and marginal cost assuming output exogeneity are quite plausible as are our scale elasticities, which are based on the output coefficient.

44. The price of capital was not significant in either specification.

45. The source of all variables is the ICC Annual Motor Carrier Reports as compiled in the American Trucking Association data tapes. The TL sector excluded household goods carriers, armored trucking, dump truckers, mine ore trucking, and retail store delivery. Following Ann F. Friedlaender and Richard H. Spady, *Freight Transport Regulation: Equity, Efficiency, and Competition in the Rail and Trucking Industries* (MIT Press, 1981), long-run total cost was measured as the sum of operating costs plus a 12 percent opportunity cost of capital, with capital measured as net operating property. In the absence of published data on route density, we approximated this variable by dividing ton miles by route miles, where route miles = $[1/2 \ n \ (n \ - \ 1) \ \cdot$ average length of haul] and n is the number of terminals. This approximation is exact if all possible routes in the network are used with equal traffic flows. Although most carriers' networks are not likely to satisfy this condition, based on a phone survey in which we asked roughly twenty carriers to estimate their route miles, the approximation error appears to be small. As an additional sensitivity test, we approximated route miles by $(n \ \cdot$ average length of haul) and found that this change had little effect on the estimated coefficient for route density. The cost functions were estimated with observations from 1985 and 1984; all variables were deflated by the GDP deflator to put the coefficients in 1977 dollars.

46. We estimated a translog cost and factor share system for motor carriers and railroads. The structural parameter estimates appeared to be reasonable, and produced plausible estimates of such measures as the scale elasticity at the sample means. But when we used the system to predict deregulated costs for individual carriers, problems arose. This is not uncommon when flexible functional forms are used to make predictions at points away from the sample mean. Steven Morrison and Clifford Winston, *The Economic Effects of Airline Deregulation* (Brookings, 1986) experienced similar difficulties when they tried to

Table 3-6. *Truckload Cost Model Parameter Estimates*[a]

Variable	Coefficient
Constant	−1.4507
	(0.3609)
Ton miles	0.9182
	(0.0100)
Average length of haul (miles)	−0.3172
	(0.0206)
Average load (tons)	−0.6179
	(0.0224)
Average compensation (dollars per year)	0.2719
	(0.0363)
Fuel price (dollars per gallon)	0.0995
	(0.0393)
Insurance expenditures (dollars per ton)	0.2369
	(0.0176)

Source: Authors' calculations.
a. $R^2 = 0.96$; number of observations = 737. Standard errors are in parentheses.

and are statistically reliable, are presented in tables 3-6 and 3-7. The results reveal operating economies from increasing length of haul, load size, and density, and some economies of pure size in TL operations.[47] The results also indicate that LTL carriers' costs increase as the share of revenue derived from LTL shipments increases. Where appropriate, the variables in each specification were deflated to 1977 dollars and all variables were multiplied by their respective coefficient to predict 1977 deregulated costs for each firm in the sample. As in the case of the rate deflator, we adjusted the LTL wage deflator to account for the impact of deregulation on wages.[48] We then deflated 1985 revenues for the TL and LTL

use a flexible functional form to make an out-of-sample prediction of deregulated airline profits. Terrence J. Wales, "On the Flexibility of Flexible Functional Forms: An Empirical Approach," *Journal of Econometrics*, vol. 5 (March 1977), pp. 183–93, provides a general discussion of this problem.

47. There were no economies of pure size in the translog specification. For a further discussion of cost structure in the deregulated motor carrier industry, see Curtis M. Grimm, Thomas M. Corsi, and Judith L. Jarrell, "U.S. Motor Carrier Cost Structure under Deregulation," *The Logistics and Transportation Review*, vol. 25 (September 1989), pp. 231–50.

48. Specific American Trucking Association deflators were used to deflate the factor prices. In addition, on the basis of Rose, "Labor Rent Sharing and Regulation," we increased the wage deflator for LTL carriers 20 percent to capture the impact of deregulation on wages.

Table 3-7.   *Less-Than-Truckload Cost Model Parameter Estimates*[a]

Variable	Coefficient
Ton miles	1.0060
	(0.0109)
Route density	−0.0630
	(0.0100)
Average load (tons)	−0.4050
	(0.0387)
Average length of haul (miles)	−0.6095
	(0.0397)
Average compensation (dollars per year)	0.2580
	(0.0243)
Fuel price (dollars per gallon)	0.2002
	(0.0525)
Insurance expenditures (dollars per ton)	0.3104
	(0.0309)
LTL revenue as a percentage of total revenue	0.1429
	(0.0233)

Source: Authors' calculations.
a. $R^2 = 0.99$; number of observations = 212. Standard errors are in parentheses.

carriers in our sample by the TL and LTL counterfactual rate deflators to obtain 1977 deregulated revenues.[49] Industry costs and revenues were then used to calculate deregulated profits and compare them with actual regulated profits.[50]

The results are presented in table 3-8. As expected, deregulation has had a small impact on the profits of truckload carriers because they have

49. The estimates of counterfactual revenues for TL carriers and rail are adjusted for the long-run trend for traffic to shift from rail to truck. Between 1977 and 1985 TL motor carrier has gained traffic from rail that is not related to deregulation, but to this trend. We therefore fit a market share trend equation and predicted what rail's market share would have been in the absence of deregulation in 1985, finding it to be a few percentage points lower than it actually was. We thus increased rail's market share and its 1985 revenues accordingly, netting out the increase in variable costs, to account for revenue losses that have occurred because of the trend. Truckload 1985 motor carrier revenues were correspondingly adjusted downward. Counterfactual 1977 revenues are based on these adjusted 1985 revenues.

50. We made deregulated industry profit estimates by inflating our sample estimates by the ratio of total revenues in the industry to the total revenues accounted for by the firms in our sample. Total costs under regulation were adjusted to maintain consistency with the opportunity cost of capital adjustment in deregulated costs.

Table 3-8. *Change in Motor Carrier and Railroad Profits Attributable to Deregulation*

Billions of 1977 dollars

Item	TL motor carriers	LTL motor carriers	Railroads
1977 regulated revenues	6.08	12.56	18.1
1977 deregulated revenues	5.96	11.92	17.6
Change	−0.12	−0.64	−0.5
1977 regulated costs	6.00	12.08	24.8
1977 deregulated costs	5.40	14.36	22.7
Change	0.60	−2.28	2.1
Change in profits	0.48	−2.92	1.6

Source: Authors' calculations.

always had to compete against a highly competitive unregulated sector.[51] Cost savings have resulted from the development of highly efficient carriers such as advanced truckload firms, leading to a $0.48 billion (1977 dollars) gain in profits from deregulation. In contrast, deregulation has lowered the annual profits of LTL carriers by $2.92 billion (1977 dollars), turning excess profits of $0.5 billion during regulation into losses of roughly $2.5 billion.[52] Revenue losses, which were expected because of increased competition, amount to $0.64 billion, while cost increases, which are somewhat surprising, total $2.28 billion. Although LTL carriers have been able to reduce labor costs, the industry has become so competitive that they have had to incur greater operating expenses and provide better service to attract and keep traffic.[53] Some of the costly service improvements are reflected in shippers' benefits from lower mean transit

51. During regulation, the TL sector contrasted sharply with the LTL sector by having far more firms and far less disciplined rate bureaus. Accordingly, although the number of firms in the TL sector has risen since deregulation, the substantial competition already in place has hardly increased.

52. This, of course, does not imply that under deregulation the LTL sector will not earn a normal return in the long run. It simply implies that under deregulation its profits will be roughly $2.9 billion less in 1977 dollars or $5.3 billion less in 1988 dollars for any given year than they would have been had the industry been regulated during that year.

53. Theodore E. Keeler, "Public Policy and Productivity in the Trucking Industry: Some Evidence on the Effects of Highway Investments, Deregulation, and the 55 MPH Speed Limit," *American Economic Review*, vol. 76 (May 1986, *Papers and Proceedings, 1985*), pp. 153–58, also finds truck deregulation increasing carrier costs.

Table 3-9. *Railroad Cost Model Parameter Estimates*[a]

Variable	Coefficient
Constant	2.1027
	(0.4824)
Ton miles	1.0023
	(0.0281)
Average length of haul (miles)	−0.3902
	(0.0565)
Density	−0.4222
	(0.0486)
Fuel price (dollars per gallon)	0.1934
	(0.1491)
Wage (dollars per hour)	0.2304
	(0.0968)

Source: Authors' calculations.
a. $R^2 = 0.93$; number of observations = 180. Standard errors are in parentheses.

times, while other improvements, which we do not measure for shippers, are reflected in more frequent service. The intense fight for traffic has also forced LTL carriers to increase their advertising expenditures and to carry lower average loads. Finally, because LTL carriers are less able to compete effectively against advanced TL firms for TL traffic, they must derive a greater share of their revenue from more costly LTL traffic.

Railroads

A log-linear rail cost specification and least squares estimation results are presented in table 3-9.[54] The parameters have the correct signs, are statistically reliable, and are consistent with previous research in finding

54. The sample consists of all Class I carriers. Data for all variables are from the Annual Report of Class I Railroads to the ICC. Total costs are defined as the sum of operating and capital costs, with capital costs based on current economic value as computed in a special unpublished study by the Depreciation Branch of the ICC. Observations were drawn from 1979–83, with all variables deflated by the GDP deflator to put the coefficients in 1977 dollars. The effect of the price of capital was small and insignificant in the log-linear model.

economies of density and length of haul but no economies of pure size.[55] The appropriate variables in this specification were deflated to 1977 dollars (the wage deflator was adjusted to account for the impact of deregulation on railroad wages), and all variables were multiplied by their respective coefficients to predict industry deregulated costs.[56] The counterfactual rail rate deflator for all commodities, 1.89, was used to deflate 1985 revenues to 1977.[57] The findings are also presented in table 3-8.

Deregulation has led to an improvement in railroad profits. The industry was actually losing $6.7 billion in 1977; had it been deregulated that year, losses would have been reduced by $1.6 billion. Railroads have improved the efficiency of their operations, lowering their costs by $2.1 billion and also enabling them to provide better service to shippers.[58] Because deregulation has enabled railroads to scale back their inefficient operations by abandonment while forcing them to compete more fiercely with each other and with motor carriers, rail revenues have suffered. Railroads have softened this loss by changing their rate structure, increasing rates where they face less competition and lowering rates where they face more, but they have not been able to extract enough shippers' surplus—especially from service improvements—to realize a revenue gain.[59]

55. This literature is reviewed in Anthony Barbera and others, "Railroad Cost Structure—Revisited," *Journal of the Transportation Research Forum,* vol. 28, no. 1 (1987), pp. 237-44.

56. Specific Association of American Railroads deflators were used to deflate the factor prices. The wage deflator was increased 20 percent, on the basis of research in the AAR Intermodal Policy Division, to account for the impact of deregulation on rail wages.

57. Rail revenues in 1985 were adjusted as described in footnotes 40 and 49. That is, 1985 rail revenues were increased to account for losses due to long-run modal and commodity shifts that are not attributable to deregulation. Real declines in coal and grain prices that are unrelated to deregulation but nonetheless could lower coal and grain rail rates (see footnote 10) cause rail revenue and profitability under deregulation to be somewhat understated. Regulated rail industry costs were adjusted to maintain consistency with the capital cost adjustments to the deregulated costs.

58. We have not mentioned the Economic Recovery Tax Act of 1981, which increased depreciation rates and shortened depreciation lives. This change helped the railroad industry, but it is difficult to determine how it should be treated here. Because our study relies on 1983 performance to determine counterfactual deregulated cost performance in 1977, the 1981 tax change may not be particularly important. To the extent that it is, one could argue that its benefits could have been reaped only in a deregulated environment. Under regulation, with the rail industry earning a 2 percent return, it is unlikely that management would have reinvested the tax savings in the industry. Under deregulation, investors' and managers' expectations about industry performance have justifiably become more optimistic, and the tax savings have been reinvested.

59. Recall that our sensitivity analysis of the effects of rail rate deregulation on shippers,

Effects on Labor and Small Communities

During the political battles over deregulation during the 1970s, some of the most vocal opponents of deregulation were unionized labor in the motor carrier industry and shippers in small communities. Both groups expected to suffer economic harm from the change in regulatory policy. The available evidence suggests that labor's fears—but not small communities'—have been realized.

Labor

It has long been argued that under regulation unionized labor in the LTL trucking sector was able to extract rents from carriers in the form of excess wages and to maintain high levels of employment. What impact has deregulation had on LTL wages and employment? Rose finds that union wages in 1977 were at least 20 percent higher than they would have been had the industry been deregulated in 1977.[60] Employment levels in the LTL sector have probably fallen because of deregulation. A factual comparison shows that LTL employment has fallen from 310,910 in 1977 to 223,061 in 1985, and a simple trend analysis suggests that some of this decline is attributable to deregulation.[61] A plausible explanation is that deregulation forced unionized labor to make work rule concessions that enabled carriers to squeeze excess capacity from their work force. Thus, not accounting for displaced workers, LTL labor has lost at least $670 million (1977 dollars) because of deregulation.

Labor in the rail industry has also suffered wage losses. The Association

---

which allowed shipment size and length of haul to change in response to deregulation and thus is consistent with the revenue analysis above, found that deregulation led, on average, to a decline in railroad rates.

60. Rose, "Labor Rent Sharing and Regulation."

61. Employment data are from ICC Annual Motor Carrier Reports. We fit a time-series regression for employment using a dummy variable for deregulation and found deregulation to have a significant negative effect. We attempted a counterfactual analysis of employment changes based on a labor demand function, but we were unable to get very reliable predictions. Nonetheless, the models we did investigate suggested employment under deregulation would have decreased. Owen, "Deregulation in the Trucking Industry," points out that total trucking industry employment rose 29 percent from 1980 to 1987. But most of the increase is in the TL sector and is most likely attributable to the economic expansion following 1982 and to the entry of unregulated carriers, such as private trucking, into the TL sector.

of American Railroads estimates that various work rule concessions and resulting improvements in labor productivity mean that wages under deregulation are at least 20 percent lower than they would be under regulation.[62] Employment has actually fallen from 482,731 in 1977 to 301,879 in 1985, but this decline appears to be part of a long-term trend and not attributable to deregulation.[63] Nonetheless, railroad labor has lost roughly $1 billion (1977 dollars) as a result of deregulation.

Service to Small Communities

Shippers in small and remote communities were concerned that motor carriers and railroads would respond to liberalized exit restrictions by abandoning service to their communities. In fact, motor carrier service to small communities has stayed constant or improved since deregulation.[64] The growth of competition in the industry has made these communities an important source of traffic for some carriers.

Railroads have abandoned thousands of miles of track since deregulation, but they have sold some of it to short-line railroads that have maintained rail service to small communities with the use of nonunion labor and have generally shown how cost-effective rail service can be. In just the past decade, the number of these small carriers has doubled.[65] Indeed, some industries have found it cost efficient to purchase track and use their labor force to provide their own rail service.[66] Thus, even with large-scale abandonments, rail service has not been extensively denied to those communities that have the traffic to support a small system.[67]

62. Association of American Railroads, Intermodal Policy Division.

63. Employment figures are from Annual Reports of Class I Carriers to the ICC. We fit a time-series regression for rail employment and found that the dummy variable for deregulation was insignificant. We again attempted a counterfactual analysis of employment changes using a labor demand function, but could not obtain reliable predictions.

64. Owen, "Deregulation in the Trucking Industry."

65. John F. Due, "Abandonment of Rail Lines and the Smaller Railroad Alternative," *Logistics and Transportation Review*, vol. 23 (March 1987), pp. 109–34.

66. Bob Secter, "Staying on Track," *Los Angeles Times*, Orange County edition, April 27, 1988, part 4, pp. 1, 12.

67. Theodore E. Keeler, *Railroads, Freight, and Public Policy* (Brookings, 1983), points out that subsidies from federal, state, and local governments have also facilitated the development of short-line railroads.

Conclusions and Qualifications

Congressional approval of the surface freight deregulation legislation in 1980 aroused considerable anxiety among all industry participants over the changes it would bring. Ten years of experience with deregulation reveal that it has conferred substantial benefits on shippers and railroads but at a cost to LTL motor carriers and to the rail and LTL motor carrier work force. Of course, the distributional effects that probably exist between small and large shippers make it very unlikely that all shippers have shared in the benefits. Shippers', and ultimately final consumers', annual benefits amount to some $20 billion (1988 dollars), and railroads' and TL carriers' annual profit gains total $2.9 billion (1988 dollars) and $0.88 billion (1988 dollars), respectively. Annual LTL carrier profit losses are estimated to be $5.3 billion (1988 dollars), and the annual losses to railroad and LTL labor are roughly $3 billion (1988 dollars), which yield an annual net welfare gain of almost $16 billion (1988 dollars).

Several assumptions that we have made and various effects of deregulation on service quality that we have not quantified suggest that benefits to shippers are probably greater than we report. We have also not taken into account the likelihood that increased competition in the surface freight industry has diverted some freight from water transport and pipeline to truck and railroads or forced rate reductions. Thus, our estimate of net welfare is certainly understated. The next issue we address is how high net welfare could be.

Chapter Four

Deregulation and Optimality

ALTHOUGH surface freight deregulation has improved economic welfare, it is unclear whether it has generated an optimal allocation of resources in freight transportation. Policymakers expected the trucking industry, thought to be inherently competitive, to achieve optimal performance under deregulation: rates would equal marginal cost and carriers would earn a normal return in the long run. Because railroads are characterized by economies of density and are sometimes able to exercise market power, marginal cost pricing was viewed as an unlikely outcome of deregulation, and rail deregulation was expected to fall short of optimal benefits.

In this chapter we estimate how close the deregulated surface freight industry as a whole has come to attaining optimal benefits. Our aim is to identify what further improvements in economic welfare could be made. We estimate the gap between shippers' and carriers' welfare under deregulation and what their welfare would be if rail and motor carrier rates were set equal to marginal cost. We then assess the prospects for achieving optimality.

Our analysis presumes that in the long run both the rail and trucking industries can reach an equilibrium characterized by marginal cost pricing. Some may question that presumption. Because railroads are characterized by economies of density, a Ramsey pricing equilibrium would appear to be more appropriate. John Meyer and William Tye, however, argue that the Ramsey equilibrium is not sustainable.[1] They envision shippers and railroads moving toward a contract equilibrium in which a tremendous amount of the excess capacity in rail operations would be removed, railroads would continue to optimize their networks, and shippers and railroads would use contracts to help railroads to become more efficient, for example, by ensuring that railroads have loads in both directions. Marginal cost pricing would emerge as a prominent feature of this equilibrium.

In assessing the overall optimality of the surface freight industry, the

1. John R. Meyer and William B. Tye, "Toward Achieving Workable Competition in Industries Undergoing a Transition to Deregulation: A Contractual Equilibrium Approach," *Yale Journal on Regulation*, vol. 5 (1988), pp. 273–97.

financial situation of the railroads must not be ignored. Although railroads have benefited significantly from deregulation, they are still not earning a normal return. Their long-run financial health must therefore be considered along with shippers' welfare.

Deregulation and Shipper Optimality

We estimate the difference between shippers' welfare under deregulation and their optimal welfare by recalculating the surplus measures for coal and grain and the CVs for the other commodities. Shippers' optimal level of welfare is determined by setting motor common carrier and rail freight charges for all shipments in our sample equal to long-run marginal cost.[2] Long-run marginal costs for each shipment were obtained from the motor carrier and rail cost models presented in chapter 3 in the following linear form:[3]

Marginal cost of a rail = − $19.06 *Route density* + $8.338 *Tons* +
shipment (dollars) $0.0164 *Ton miles*

Marginal cost of a TL = − $0.495 *Average load* − $0.004 *Average*
shipment (dollars)   *length of haul* + $0.056 *Ton miles*

Marginal cost of an LTL = − $1.673 *Average load* − $0.053 *Average*
shipment (dollars)   *length of haul* + $0.212 *Ton miles.*

For representative movements, these equations predict the marginal cost of rail to be 2.0–3.0 cents per ton mile, the marginal cost of TL motor

2. We attempted to include rail service quality in our welfare measure and to optimize rates and service simultaneously. Unfortunately, there are no estimates of the relation between rail costs and service time that vary by car type. We performed some calculations assuming that the elasticity of costs with respect to service time was 1.0 and found that optimization of service, adjusting rates to reflect the improved service, did not significantly affect the deregulated service-rate trade-off.

3. Each shipment's weight (tons) and length of haul (miles) was substituted into the equations to predict its marginal cost. For the coal and grain commodities, rail's marginal cost was adjusted using a bulk commodities deflator based on findings in Ann F. Friedlaender and Richard H. Spady, *Freight Transport Regulation: Equity, Efficiency, and Competition in the Rail and Trucking Industries* (MIT Press, 1981). Because rail route density is defined as ton miles divided by route miles, we set route miles equal to the average route miles in the industry.

carrier to be 4.5–5.5 cents per ton mile, and the marginal cost of LTL motor carrier to be 15–19 cents per ton mile, all plausible estimates.[4]

Using these equations to predict marginal costs, we recalculated the CVs and surplus measures and found that deregulated welfare fell short of optimal welfare by $0.69 billion (1977 dollars) for rail shipments of coal and grain and by $4.91 billion (1977 dollars) for movements of the other commodities, with the gap in the latter case almost entirely due to rail rates. Thus, deregulation has led to optimality in motor carrier pricing, but has fallen short of attaining optimality for shippers in rail pricing by nearly $6 billion.

The net welfare gain to society from marginal cost pricing, however, is small because the loss in railroad profits is only $0.23 billion less than the welfare gain to shippers. This gain is lower than the welfare gain from marginal cost pricing under regulation because deregulation itself has eliminated the loss in the motor carrier sector and because rail's distortions have become more optimal: rate distortions are greater for the inelastic shipments and lower for the elastic shipments.

Although marginal cost pricing would generate significant benefits to shippers, it would be harmful to the rail industry in its present form. The appropriate policies under the circumstances would be to promote competition to improve shipper welfare and to promote efficiency to improve rail's financial performance. We reserve discussion of these policies until chapter 5. First, we demonstrate the impact that more rail competition could have on shippers' welfare, and then identify areas where greater railroad efficiency could substantially increase their profits.

Competition and Welfare under Deregulation

One way to lower rates and improve shippers' welfare is to generate more competition in rail transportation. Analysts, however, disagree as to the importance of competition within the rail industry. The issue has been debated in recent rail merger cases, with merger applicants stressing the importance of competition between the rail and trucking industries, as well as product and source competition, and merger opponents arguing that competition within the rail industry itself is quite important. The ICC

4. These estimates are in counterfactual deregulated (1977) dollars.

Figure 4-1. *Single-Line and Interline Competitors*

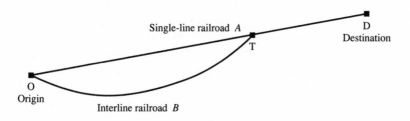

has typically defined the relevant transportation market as rail freight transportation only.[5]

Competition could come in two forms, single-line and interline rail service. As shown in figure 4-1, a single-line carrier serves the entire route O–D. The interline carrier serves the origin and part of the route, O–T, and then transfers the shipment to another railroad to complete the rest of the movement, T–D. The role of interline competitors has been particularly contentious, especially in situations such as figure 4-1, where a single-line railroad holds a monopoly over one segment of the market. In theory, a monopolist over one link of the production chain can fully exploit that monopoly power by "price squeezing" upstream or downstream firms. With reference to figure 4-1, railroad A would price squeeze railroad B by insisting on a large enough division of joint-line revenues to realize full monopoly profits and render the interline competition of railroad B ineffectual. In practice, however, there are restrictions on such price squeezes in the railroad industry. Revenue divisions over interline traffic are typically governed by industry standard division rules, which set divisions according to mileage or other proxies to relative marginal costs. There is a clear efficiency rationale for establishing such standard divisions, since it eliminates having to negotiate individual divisions over thousands of routings and markets. Moreover, a carrier in the position of railroad A is deterred from deviating from standard divisions in an effort to price squeeze railroad B by the prospect that their situations may well be reversed in many other markets. There also remain legal restrictions on the ability of a railroad with a monopoly position to price squeeze or

5. This decision has been largely based on estimates of a low cross-elasticity of demand between rail and truck. Russell W. Pittman, "Railroads and Competition: the Santa Fe/ Southern Pacific Merger Proposal," *Journal of Industrial Economics* (forthcoming).

refuse to deal with interline competitors. ICC regulatory oversight, and perhaps more important, the prospect of antitrust actions for attempted monopolization, deter the exercise of full monopoly power.[6]

Interline competitors such as railroad B can thus provide effective competition. Shippers can use the threat of shipping via the interline route to gain leverage in negotiating with the single-line carrier. In addition, interline carriers can offer confidential contracts rebating a portion of revenues to shippers who choose the interline routing.[7] One way to resolve the conflict between predictions of the effect of interline competitors generated from pure theory and those taking into account rail practice is to test empirically the role of interline competitors in reducing rates and increasing shipper welfare.[8]

We estimate the effect of single-line and interline rail competition on the difference between shippers' deregulated and optimal welfare, ΔW, for all our shipments.[9] The CVs and surplus measure used to obtain the

6. For a more detailed discussion of both the relevant theory and institutional factors in the railroad industry, see Henry McFarland, "The Economics of Vertical Restraints and Relationships between Connecting Railroads," *Logistics and Transportation Review,* vol. 23 (June 1986), pp. 207–22; Curtis M. Grimm and Robert G. Harris, "Vertical Foreclosure in the Rail Freight Industry: Economic Analysis and Policy Prescriptions," *ICC Practitioners' Journal,* vol. 50 (July–August 1983), pp. 508–31; Curtis M. Grimm and Robert G. Harris, "A Qualitative Choice Analysis of Rail Routings: Implications for Vertical Foreclosure and Competition Policy," *Logistics and Transportation Review,* vol. 24 (March 1988); and William B. Tye, "Post-Merger Denials of Competitive Access and Trackage Rights in the Rail Industry," *Transportation Practitioners' Journal,* vol. 53, no. 4 (1986), pp. 413–27. See also Alfred E. Kahn, *The Economics of Regulation: Principles and Institutions,* vol. 2 (John Wiley, 1970), pp. 64–70 and 307–23; and Jean Tirole, *The Theory of Industrial Organization* (MIT Press, 1988), pp. 193–201, for a discussion of the relevant economic theory. An example of antitrust action relating to railroad local monopoly power is *Grand Trunk Western* v. *Conrail,* Civil Action Number 84-CV-2359-DT, which was settled out of court.

7. Rail shippers have long argued that the existence of interline competitors is of value in obtaining lower rates. See, for example, Interstate Commerce Commission *Ex Parte* no. 445, July 7, 1983, p. 10, and Interstate Commerce Commission *Ex Parte* no. 427, "Petition of The National Industrial Transportation League," February 25, 1983, p. 7.

8. Previous evidence on the value of rail competition in general is provided by Richard C. Levin, "Railroad Rates, Profitability, and Welfare under Deregulation," *Bell Journal of Economics,* vol. 12 (Spring 1981), pp. 1–26; and Curtis M. Grimm, "Horizontal Competitive Effects in Railroad Mergers," in Theodore E. Keeler, ed., *Research in Transportation Economics,* vol. 2 (1985), pp. 27–53.

9. Single-line and interline rail competitors, where interline competitors are defined as serving the origin and part of the route, are derived from the Economics and Finance Department, Association of American Railroads, *Rail Stations by Standard Point Location Codes* (Washington, January 1986). Alternate definitions of interline carriers, such as carriers that serve any segment of the route, did not improve upon results.

aggregate estimate of this difference were used to construct this variable. Because of the substantial capital required to enter the rail industry, it is reasonable to assume that single-line and interline competitors are exogenous in this model. Although the source of ΔW is from rail, truckload motor carriers could have an important effect. But because most TL carriers are independent and do not have fixed networks, this effect is difficult to measure and, in fact, may not vary substantially across markets. Thus, we do not explicitly include it. We do include shipment size and distance in the specification. Both variables could capture features of carriers' rate schedules and the unmeasured effect of competition between rail and truck. Larger shipment sizes and distances are more likely to be rail-truck competitive and thus lower ΔW. Finally, we control for any variation in effects by commodity with commodity dummies.[10]

We estimated separate models for each commodity group and found that it was statistically justified to combine shipments and estimate one model for coal and grain and one for all other commodity groups. Least squares estimation results are presented in table 4-1. For all commodity groups except coal and grain the impact of single-line and interline rail competitors on shippers' welfare is substantial. One additional single-line rail competitor reduces the welfare difference by 9.1 cents per ton mile; one additional interline competitor reduces the difference by 3.4 cents per ton mile.[11] Either addition would eliminate the welfare gap faced by shippers, which averages less than 1 cent per ton mile. Interestingly, the relative impact of single-line and interline rail competitors on welfare, nearly three to one, is virtually the same as in airlines.[12]

It is easy to understand why one additional rail competitor would have such an enormous impact on shipper welfare: virtually no large carriers

10. We also attempted to control for competition supplied by water carrier and for density effects using dummy variables. But these variables were statistically insignificant. A more precise measure of the effect of water competition, the shipper's distance from a freight-carrying waterway, was not available.

11. We investigated whether the impact of interline competitors varied with the presence of a single-line competitor on the route. We interacted interline competitors with a dummy variable to capture the impact of interline competitors both when there were and when there were not single-line competitors on the route. The coefficients for these variables were not statistically significantly different.

12. A potential competitor in airlines could fit the definition of interline competitors in rail. Steven A. Morrison and Clifford Winston, "Empirical Implications and Tests of the Contestability Hypothesis," *Journal of Law and Economics,* vol. 30 (April 1987), pp. 53–66, find potential carriers have roughly one-third of the impact on welfare as actual airline carriers.

Table 4-1. Welfare Difference Parameter Estimates[a]

| | Coefficient | |
| | --- | --- |
Variable	All commodities excluding coal and grain[b]	Coal and grain[c]
Constant	−128.5340	0.1541
	(37.6816)	(0.1403)
One-way distance (miles)	0.7732	0.0121
	(0.0729)	(0.0005)
One-way distance squared (miles)	-0.2494×10^{-3}	-0.0060×10^{-3}
	$(0.0269) \times 10^{-3}$	$(0.0004) \times 10^{-3}$
Single-line rail competitors interacted with distance	−0.0915	−0.0010
	(0.0141)	(0.0001)
Interline rail competitors interacted with distance	−0.0339	−0.0007
	(0.0073)	(0.0001)
Shipment weight (thousands of pounds)	−2.3338	−0.0002
	(0.6917)	(0.0001)
Metal commodity dummy	208.4140	. . .
	(36.3301)	
Petroleum commodity dummy	138.1640	. . .
	(136.5610)	
Glass commodity dummy	265.8230	. . .
	(38.8240)	
Plastic commodity dummy	172.8850	. . .
	(74.0027)	
Coal dummy	. . .	−0.8407
		(0.1080)

Source: Authors' calculations.
a. Dependent variable is welfare difference per ton.
b. $R^2 = 0.19$; number of observations = 1,210. Standard errors are in parentheses. Interline competitiors only include Class I carriers.
c. $R^2 = 0.33$; number of observations = 1,588. Standard errors are in parentheses. Interline competitors include all carriers.

have entered the industry for nearly a century. New entry requires the construction of a prohibitively expensive new network. A railroad planning a medium-sized network of 5,000 track miles would need more than several billion dollars to enter the industry. Entry by existing carriers is less difficult, but still requires construction of track and acquisition of right-of-way for markets the carrier wants to enter.[13] As a result, the

13. Entry can occur in special situations, such as the Union Pacific–C&NW line into the Powder River Basin coal mining area of Wyoming.

shortage of competition at the route level is dramatic. Currently, for all commodities except grain and coal there is, on average, slightly more than one (1.15, based on our sample) single-line carrier and slightly fewer than two (1.78) interline carriers in a market.[14]

Rail competition has far less impact on shippers' welfare in coal and grain markets.[15] One additional single-line competitor reduces the welfare difference by 0.1 cent per ton mile; one additional interline competitor reduces the difference by 0.07 cent per ton mile. Thus, an additional single-line rail competitor lowers the welfare difference by roughly 10 percent, which still leaves a substantial gap. What accounts for such a large difference between the effect of rail competition across commodity groups? Coal and grain differ from other commodities in a number of respects. They are still subject to ICC regulatory review, and a large fraction of their shipments moves under contract rates. The regulatory environment could effectively enable carriers to engage in more coordination (tacit collusion) and less competition than would be the case under full deregulation. And shippers' commitment to long-term contracts (some coal contracts run for ten years) could limit their response to changes in competition. Further, the effects of changes in rail competition in coal and grain markets may be constrained by external factors such as source or product competition in coal and unregulated motor carriers in grain.

Benefits to Railroads and Shippers from Further Adjustments to Deregulation

It is important to recognize that carriers are still adjusting to deregulation and that further welfare gains to shippers and carriers are still possible without changes in public policy.

Shippers could increase benefits by improving their contracting with railroads. By providing railroads with a volume commitment and matching loads (loads in both directions), they can help lower railroads' costs, increase their own bargaining power, and obtain lower contract rates. As

14. The figures for coal and grain commodities are 1.53 single-line competitors and 0.86 interline competitors. (Interline competitors are defined as serving the origin and part of the route.) Authors' calculations based on the Economics and Finance Department, Association of American Railroads, *Rail Station by Standard Point Location Codes,* and the 1985 ICC Waybill Tapes.

15. This conclusion persisted when we estimated separate models for coal and grain.

Table 4-2. *Changes in Railroad Costs Due to Changes in Operating Efficiency and Labor Costs*[a]

Billions of 1977 dollars

Change	Railroad costs
Base case	22.71
Increase in operating efficiency	
10 percent	21.01
20 percent	19.58
50 percent	16.34
Combined increase in operating efficiency and decrease in labor costs	
10 percent	20.51
20 percent	18.60
50 percent	13.92

Source: Authors' calculations.
a. Operating efficiency changes include changes in density and length of haul.

suggested by our sensitivity analysis in chapter 3, if shippers negotiated the lowest contract rate available, they would receive almost $2 billion in benefits.

Railroads are just beginning to introduce technological innovations such as computerized dispatching systems and sophisticated scheduling practices that use equipment and labor more efficiently. In addition, further compromises from unions could modify costly work rules, while further abandonment of unprofitable branch lines would also improve profits.[16] In table 4-2, we use our railroad cost function to show how railroad costs would be affected by increased operating efficiencies in the form of higher densities and longer lengths of haul. A 20 percent *increase* leads to a $3 billion cost reduction. A more drastic increase, 50 percent, results in more than a $6 billion saving, which would eliminate the actual and counterfactual profit loss for 1977.[17] If these operating efficiencies are complemented by labor cost savings, the cost reductions are even greater. Railroads could also realize profit gains from further infusion of more dynamic and better educated managers who are able to improve railroad operations. It

16. Curtis M. Grimm, "Excess Branch Line Capacity in the U.S. Railroad Industry: A Simulation Model Approach," *Logistics and Transportation Review*, vol. 22 (September 1986), pp. 223–40, finds that substantial railroad excess capacity still remains. Depending primarily on assumptions regarding fixed costs, there were estimated to be 20,000–50,000 miles of unprofitable Class I light-density lines as of the mid-1980s.

17. Because there may be revenue losses from the abandonment of light-density lines, the cost savings overstate the gain in profits.

has long been argued that a major cost of regulation has been its effect on the rail industry's ability, or perhaps willingness, to recruit high-quality management.[18]

Conclusion

Although the net welfare gain from marginal cost pricing in the de-regulated surface freight transportation industry is small, shippers stand to reap substantial benefits from increased competition among railroads. Railroads can improve their financial performance under deregulation by operating more efficiently, reducing their labor costs, and continuing to attract higher-quality managers. Policymakers would do well to monitor industry profitability and rate levels carefully before resorting to dramatic policy changes to improve shipper welfare and rail profitability.

Indeed, further benefits from deregulation may have already been re-alized. Since 1985, average rail revenue per ton has declined in nominal terms, and in 1988 railroads earned an 8 percent return on investment, the best performance in their modern history. The remaining question is what public policy can do to help.

18. D. Daryl Wyckoff, *Railroad Management* (Lexington Books, 1976); and Robert G. Harris and Curtis M. Grimm, "Revitalisation of the U.S. Rail Freight Industry: An Organisational Perspective," in K. J. Button and D. E. Pitfield, eds., *International Railway Economics: Studies in Management and Efficiency* (Hants., England: Gower Publishing Co., 1985). Curtis M. Grimm, James A. Kling, and Ken G. Smith, "The Impact of U.S. Rail Regulatory Reform on Railroad Management and Organizational Structure," *Transportation Research*, vol. 21A (March 1987), pp. 87–94, provide evidence that the movement to a deregulated structure is affecting management characteristics. Railroad managers in 1983 were younger, had fewer years of company service, and were significantly better educated than railroad managers in 1977.

Chapter Five

Railroad and Motor Carrier Policy Issues

DEREGULATION has enhanced the efficiency of railroad and trucking operations and produced substantial benefits for shippers. The aim of public policy now should be to preserve and even increase the welfare gains from each industry. A number of the issues we touch upon in this chapter have already received much attention and could by themselves be the subject of a book. Our objective is to indicate policy directions consistent with the main thrust of our findings.

Railroad Policy Issues

Any vision of public policy toward the railroad industry must address a fundamental dilemma. Further efforts to help those shippers who are, despite deregulation, still forced to pay high rates could put the railroads in financial jeopardy. Indeed, whether the railroad industry will survive at a reasonable size is still a question. Our findings show, however, that market forces can address both these concerns. Given negotiating flexibility, shippers can and have obtained reasonable rates and improved service. Given operating freedom, railroads can and have eliminated gross inefficiencies and earned a higher return. Further progress needs to be made. The role of public policy should be to preserve and enhance Staggers Act benefits by encouraging greater railroad efficiency and by promoting rail competition.

Enhancing Railroad Efficiency

Public policy should encourage railroads to further reduce excess capacity, improve labor productivity, and increase the efficiency of freight car utilization. These areas are still a source of conspicuous inefficiencies.

Of paramount importance is that there be no new restrictions on railroads' ability to abandon routes. Recent legislative proposals to restrict abandonment, mainly prompted by Midwestern agriculture states where the excess capacity problem is most severe, must be resisted. Railroads should continue to have freedom to downsize.[1]

Railroads have increasingly spun off unprofitable lines to new short-line or regional railroads, thus preserving service to the communities involved while simultaneously eliminating a financial burden. The key to the success of the short lines is their ability to operate without restrictive work rules. So far the ICC has not imposed labor protection conditions on short-line sales. But unions have attempted to challenge this ICC action in court and have pressed for new legislation that would impose union rules on short lines. It is important that short lines continue to be allowed to use labor efficiently and without restrictions.

Use of market forces could improve the efficiency of freight car use. A railroad must pay a set per diem charge when another railroad's car is on its line. To minimize these charges, railroads will frequently try to get another railroad's car off its line as quickly as possible. As a result, circuitous routing of cars and the number of empty freight car miles increase. Greater use of market forces to determine freight car rates and usage could enhance efficiency, especially because rail cars would be directed to locations where they are most needed to haul freight.[2]

Promoting and Preserving Competition

Our findings in chapter 4 show that increased competition within the rail industry itself is important in preserving and extending the benefits from railroad deregulation. As a result of more than fifty railroad mergers since 1957, the seven largest rail systems now account for approximately 80 percent of Class I mileage and revenues. Past ICC rail merger policy has not effectively preserved rail competition. In the 1960s and 1970s, the ICC approved several major parallel mergers (for example, Seaboard

1. The only desirable restriction should be to continue to offer first priority of acquisition to persons seeking to operate the abandoned rail line.

2. For a full critique of this perverse system, see Christopher C. Barnekov, "The Track Record," *Regulation*, no. 1 (1987), pp. 19–27. See Alain L. Kornhauser, "Quantified Opportunities for Centralized Nationwide Management of Empty Freight Cars," *Transportation Research Forum*, Proceedings of the Twenty-fourth Annual Meeting, vol. 24, no. 1 (1983), pp. 140–53, for further information on potential cost savings from more efficient freight car management. The ICC has initiated *Ex Parte* 334 Sub. 6 to solicit comments on reforming the present system of per diem car hire charges.

Figure 5-1. *Vertical Foreclosure*

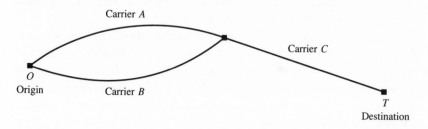

Coast Line, Penn Central, and Burlington Northern) that resulted in rail monopolies or near monopolies in large regions of the country.[3] Recent years have seen another round of rail consolidations. Four major end-to-end mergers were approved by the ICC in the early 1980s. The ICC did deny, however, a largely parallel merger between the Santa Fe and Southern Pacific railroads.

As Alfred Kahn and others have noted of the airline industry, it is important to recognize that deregulation did not authorize the government to abdicate its antitrust responsibility and to fail to take actions to preserve competition. To the extent that mergers can enable railroads to improve service and reduce costs without concomitant anticompetitive effects, they should be encouraged. It is the ICC's responsibility to scrutinize carefully potential anticompetitive effects from both parallel and end-to-end mergers. In particular, a policy of continuing to discourage parallel mergers appears to be in order. Analysis by Russell Pittman confirms that the loss of competition from the Santa Fe/Southern Pacific merger would have been substantial, with deadweight losses in the range of $75–100 million.[4]

Although end-to-end consolidations do not have the salient anticompetitive effects of parallel mergers, they may nonetheless pose competitive problems, namely vertical foreclosure of nonmerging carriers. Figure 5-1 illustrates this issue. If carriers *A* and *C* merge, carrier *B* may be foreclosed

3. Theodore E. Keeler, *Railroads, Freight, and Public Policy* (Brookings, 1983), p. 37.

4. Russell Pittman, "Railroads and Competition: Why the Santa Fe/Southern Pacific Merger Had to Die," Department of Justice Economic Analysis Group Discussion Paper, EAG 88-10, August 26, 1988. Evidence of increased rates from parallel mergers is also provided in Curtis M. Grimm, "Horizontal Competitive Effects in Railroad Mergers," in Theodore E. Keeler, ed., *Research in Transportation Economics*, vol. 2 (1985), pp. 27–53.

from participation in movements from *O* to *T* or may be price squeezed by the merged carrier.[5] Our empirical findings in chapter 4 indicate that effectively eliminating an interline carrier from the *O–T* market would cause a substantial loss in welfare to shippers. In recent decisions, the ICC has attached very few conditions to allow nonmerging carriers to compete effectively with merged rivals. One desirable condition would be to allow carrier *B* to have trackage rights over carrier *C*'s line, thus preserving carrier *B*'s ability to compete in the *O–T* market.[6] We recommend more vigorous application of procompetitive conditions to ameliorate vertical foreclosure in subsequent end-to-end merger cases.

The vertical foreclosure issue also arises with regard to joint rate and route cancellations. A flurry of such cancellations occurred in the first few years after passage of the Staggers Act, with Conrail, Southern Pacific, and the Seaboard System most active. The ICC's policy has been quite liberal, allowing proposed cancellations in almost all situations. Because interline competitors have an important impact on rates and economic welfare, the ICC should pursue a more restrictive policy, weighing possible anticompetitive consequences if carriers with little bargaining power are disadvantaged or eliminated from providing effective competition.[7]

A third area where the ICC should more aggressively promote competition under existing legislation involves reciprocal switching. A reciprocal switching agreement allows traffic originating on a rival carrier's tracks to be switched to another carrier in the area. Local monopoly, in which a shipper is served by only a single railroad, is perhaps the most serious structural feature that limits rail competition. Congress recognized

---

5. For a more extensive discussion of the vertical foreclosure issue, see Curtis M. Grimm and Robert G. Harris, "Vertical Foreclosure in the Rail Freight Industry: Economic Analysis and Policy Prescriptions," *ICC Practitioners' Journal*, vol. 50 (July–August 1983), pp. 508–31; and Curtis M. Grimm and Robert G. Harris, "A Qualitative Choice Analysis of Rail Routings: Implications for Vertical Foreclosure and Competition Policy," *Logistics and Transportation Review*, vol. 24 (March 1988).

6. It should be noted that such conditions could entail loss of density economies in the market, in that such economies result from lower operating costs as well as the spreading of fixed facility costs over a larger traffic base. For further details, see Robert G. Harris, "Economies of Traffic Density in the Rail Freight Industry," *Bell Journal of Economics*, vol. 8 (Autumn 1977), pp. 556–64.

7. We are not advocating a return to the overly restrictive DT&I-type conditions, wherein all interline routes, even extremely circuitous ones, were protected by ICC fiat. For more details on the dimensions of a rational, case-by-case approach to analyzing vertical foreclosure concerns in route cancellations and end-to-end mergers, see Grimm and Harris, "Vertical Foreclosure in the Rail Freight Industry," pp. 522–31.

that local monopoly power could limit the benefits of rail deregulation and included the following provision in the Staggers Act (section 223):

> The Commission may require rail carriers to enter into reciprocal switching agreements, where it finds such agreements to be practicable and in the public interest, or where such agreements are necessary to provide competitive rail service. The carriers entering into such an agreement shall establish the conditions and compensation applicable to such agreement, but if the carriers cannot agree upon such conditions and compensation within a reasonable period of time, the Commission may establish such conditions and compensation.

The ICC, however, has been reluctant to impose reciprocal switching under the Staggers Act.[8] We advocate a more active policy to promote competition in the face of local monopoly power.

Although a full discussion of ICC policy in this area is beyond the scope of this monograph, two comments are in order. First, we are advocating that reciprocal switching be imposed only when a shipper has access to just one railroad and when a second railroad is present a short distance away. Second, it is clear that imposing reciprocal switching is meaningless unless a reasonable rate for access is mandated by the ICC. However, determining such charges, based on marginal costs and an appropriate percentage of fixed costs, would not be unduly onerous and certainly would be far easier than assessing stand-alone costs under present maximum rate standards.

Contingency Plan

The preceding actions to preserve and promote competition under existing legislation could protect and enhance the benefits of deregulation. In addition, they could reduce the scope of ICC maximum rate regulation, replacing ICC mandated maximum rates with market determination of prices.[9] The captive shipper problem would also be expected to diminish

---

8. See in particular the Midtec Decision, Interstate Commerce Commission no. 39021, *Midtec Paper Corporation et al.* v. *Chicago and North Western Transportation Company,* decided December 2, 1986.

9. The ICC has in recent years abandoned Fully-Distributed-Cost pricing for coal and other captive traffic and replaced it with Ramsey pricing in principle, subject to the Stand-Alone Cost Test. As of this writing, it is still unclear precisely how the ICC will implement

over time as shippers adjust to deregulation. For example, a coal-burning electric utility might retool to use alternative fuels, thus using product competition to bargain for lower transportation rates. In addition, a utility contemplating a new plant location or expansion could sign long-term transportation contracts before committing to new investment, thus exploiting ex ante competitive alternatives.

But if the captive shipper problem becomes unexpectedly more severe, it may be appropriate to enact new legislation that separates ownership of the track from provision of service to a far greater degree than currently envisioned. One approach, recently taken by Canada, would be to guarantee blanket competitive access. Canada's National Transportation Act of 1987 provides an interswitching zone of thirty kilometers, whereby a shipper captive to railroad *A* but located within thirty kilometers of railroad *B* can ship via railroad *B*. Railroad *B* would pay railroad *A* a predetermined access charge, which varies according to distance and number of cars, thus eliminating the need for case-by-case determination of access costs. The Canadian legislation also provides for so-called competitive line rates, which allow for establishment by the national regulatory agency of a rate to the nearest interchange point. The aim of the legislation is to ensure that all shippers effectively have service by at least two competing railroads.[10]

A more serious contingency under which government action would be required is financial collapse of the railroad industry. Current trends in earnings are positive for the industry, and all but a few weak carriers should be able to withstand a moderate recession.[11] Nonetheless, a future

---

this complex new test. In any event, reducing the scope of maximum rate regulation would appear to be the best long-term solution to the current problem of implementing the Stand-Alone Cost Test. For example, according to data from a recent study on the location of coal-powered utility plants, 77 percent of those plants are located within twenty-five miles of more than one railroad. Moreover, 23 percent of these utilities are served by only one railroad but have at least one other railroad within twenty-five miles, suggesting that greater competitive access through reciprocal switching could significantly reduce the captive shipper problem.

10. Maria Rehner, "An Overview of the Rail Provisions in the National Transportation Act, 1987," *Transportation Practitioners' Journal*, vol. 55, no. 4 (1988), pp. 328–41, provides further details on the Canadian legislation. More radical proposals would allow access over all rail lines to any qualified user, including motor carriers and shippers. Recent legislation by the state of West Virginia declares railroads in the state to be public highways free to all.

11. Returns on investment for 1988 for the six largest rail systems, calculated on a consistent basis with previous year's revenue adequacy cases, are as follows: Norfolk-

financial collapse of a large portion of the railroad industry is not beyond the realm of possibility. A combination of developments, including an extended economic downturn, a serious decline in the demand for coal, major new improvements in motor carrier efficiency (perhaps from legislation easing size and weight restrictions), dramatic structural changes in the economy away from manufactured goods, and widespread implementation of new technologies such as coal slurry pipelines, could spell serious financial difficulty for the industry that should not simply be resolved by bankruptcy proceedings.[12] Such a contingency would require consideration of a more radical proposal: separating ownership of the rail infrastructure from railroad operations and allowing open access to all carriers.[13]

Under this emergency contingency plan, the government would purchase the track and set up a private corporation to administer access operations.[14] Open access could transform the cost structure of the industry, exhausting economies of density at the firm level and creating a competitive industry similar to trucking. Railroads would not face any infrastructure entry or exit barriers and would be free to serve any markets they wish. Rail rates should be fully deregulated, and the increase in competition resulting from these drastically lower entry requirements should drive rates to marginal cost.

At the same time, relieving railroads of their infrastructure obligations would reduce their costs, even though they would pay efficient access charges, by enabling them to optimize their network, which will lead to higher traffic densities and longer lengths of haul. Increased competition would force further concessions by unions and put downward pressure on labor costs. The result of these changes in cost structure, technology, and competition is that railroads should earn a normal profit in the long run.

Southern, 12.4 percent; Burlington Northern, 11.0 percent; Union Pacific, 10.9 percent; CSX, 5.8 percent; Conrail, 5.2 percent; and Southern Pacific, −2.3 percent. Thus, only Southern Pacific would appear to be in any serious financial difficulty in the event of an economic downturn.

12. The costs of preserving a private rail industry will be exceeded by the benefits. According to our shipper welfare models, the annual loss to shippers from eliminating rail as an alternative approaches $50 billion (1977 dollars).

13. A similar system—public ownership of railroad infrastructure with private companies operating with open access—has been proposed in Britain as a means of privatization. See "The Great Rail Sale," *Local Transport Today,* July 26, 1989, pp. 8–9.

14. This option was considered by the United States Railway Association, *Preliminary System Plan,* vol. 1 (Washington, February 26, 1975), in the case of Conrail. The separate rail facilities were to be called Confac.

Finally, a radically transformed railroad track network, in which unprofitable and lightly used lines were sold off, could enable the enterprise that manages the rail infrastructure to break even by setting efficient marginal cost track user charges. Thus, under the contingency of wholesale industry financial collapse, separating track ownership and rail operations may provide an attractive alternative to industry nationalization.

To be sure, a number of problems would need to be addressed before such a policy could be implemented. These include:

—financing the purchase of the railroads' infrastructure assets, whose market value was recently estimated by the ICC at $154 billion for track and physical structure and $60 billion for right-of-way;

—overcoming political opposition to increased government involvement in the economy and railroad opposition to confiscation of property;

—determining proper investment and disinvestment policies;

—pricing railroad infrastructure efficiently;

—ensuring efficient management of the infrastructure, including maintenance and construction of new track; and

—coordinating operations of multiple users safely and efficiently.

Although these problems are not to be taken lightly, solutions could be found. Future research should investigate this option in more detail so that it could be implemented if it were to become necessary.

Motor Carrier Policy Issues

Our findings suggest no compelling need for policymakers to enhance performance in the deregulated motor carrier industry. But public policy could generate benefits by ensuring that all motor carrier rates are set under fully competitive conditions, by promoting motor carrier safety, and by instituting efficient pricing of and investment in highways.

Full Deregulation of Inter- and Intrastate Freight Rates

Under the provisions of the Motor Carrier Act of 1980, interstate motor carriers are still regulated to the extent that they must still file tariffs with the ICC. Because deregulation has essentially produced the optimal level of motor carrier rates, it is difficult to argue that full deregulation of interstate rates could produce much additional benefit. Nonetheless, filing tariffs at the ICC involves unnecessary administrative work that should be eliminated, especially because it provides no protection for the shipping public against pricing abuses. Only on rare occasions are the tariffs at the ICC consulted by the shipping public or subjected to ICC review.[15]

Regulation of intrastate motor carrier rates has also been a cause for concern. Forty-one states still have some form of rate regulation unaffected by the Motor Carrier Act of 1980.[16] It has been argued that deregulation of intrastate trucking rates would have economic effects comparable to those of interstate trucking deregulation and lead to lower rates. We estimated the economic effect of deregulating intrastate rates by using our less-than-truckload rate equation to predict deregulated rates for individual intrastate movements.[17] We obtained sixty LTL intrastate shipments from California and Nebraska and found that the predicted deregulated rates were 30 percent lower than the actual regulated rates, which amounts to at least a $1.2 billion (1977 dollars) aggregate gain to shippers from intrastate rate deregulation.[18] The benefits would actually be greater because shippers would reduce any inefficiencies they incurred in plant location and shipping patterns to avoid excessive intrastate rates. The issue of states' rights is likely to be raised if federal legislation is used to deregulate intrastate motor carrier rates. But excessive rates caused by state regulation affect interstate commerce and the nation's productivity. Perhaps this perspective can elevate the issue's domain beyond state borders.

Removing Antitrust Immunity for Rate Bureaus

Although the Motor Carrier Act of 1980 placed restrictions on the activities of motor carrier rate bureaus, especially prohibiting discussion

15. Although the ICC's Certificate of Public Convenience and Necessity currently does not represent any entry barrier, entry should also be fully deregulated except for requirements to establish insurance certification for safety purposes.

16. California Public Utilities Commission, Division of Ratepayer Advocates, "Report on General Freight Regulation in California, and Program Proposals," case 1.88-08-046, October 27, 1988, p. 63.

17. Actual shipments and regulated rates were obtained from state public utility commissions. We did not find any appreciable effects from intrastate deregulation in the truckload sector. This could be because of competition supplied by the unregulated TL sector.

18. The aggregate estimate was obtained by using Eno Foundation for Transportation, Inc., *Transportation in America: A Statistical Analysis of Transportation in the United States*, 7th ed. (Westport, Conn., May 1989), p. 5, to estimate the revenue accounted for by the regulated intrastate LTL sector ($4.04 billion in 1977 dollars), and by multiplying this figure by the average reduction in rates (30 percent) to obtain a lower-bound welfare gain. Other studies confirm that intrastate rate deregulation would lead to a substantial reduction in intrastate rates. For example, Martha M. Hamilton, "ICC Limits Texas' Regulation of Rates for Stopover Freight," *Washington Post*, April 24, 1988, reports an estimated rate reduction of 38 percent for Texas.

or votes on single-line rates, it did not abolish the bureaus' antitrust immunity, creating instead the Motor Carrier Ratemaking Study Commission to examine the need for continuing immunity. The commission found that "collective ratemaking conflicts sharply with the National Transportation Policy which, as a result of the Motor Carrier Act of 1980, now calls for greater reliance on marketplace competition and, more specifically, for rate and service differentiation to meet changing market demands and the diverse requirements of the shipping public."[19] The commission recommended total elimination of antitrust immunity for collective ratemaking for all rates, for freight classification, and for related activities in the motor carrier industry.

Despite that recommendation, antitrust immunity for collective ratemaking has been removed only for single-line rates as mandated by the Motor Carrier Act. We recommend that carriers be barred from participating in all forms of collective ratemaking, including joint-line rates and general rate changes.[20] In contrast to rail, the absence of entry barriers makes joint-line rates unnecessary. In the current environment, continued antitrust immunity for rate bureaus serves no useful purpose. Carriers now provide rate diskettes directly to shippers who can access the carrier's entire tariff from their own personal computers. Shippers therefore have easy access to pricing information from a number of carriers. In addition, collective ratemaking represents a potential threat to deregulation's gains, especially in the LTL industry, where growing concentration may facilitate anticompetitive actions if immunity is continued.[21]

Safety

A chief concern of policymakers when the trucking industry was deregulated was that the increased competition would cause many carriers not

19. Motor Carrier Ratemaking Study Commission, *Collective Ratemaking in the Trucking Industry*, A Report to the President and the Congress of the United States (Washington, June 1, 1983), p. xii.

20. Following the commission's recommendations, several collective activities could be allowed, including collective tariff publication; establishment of uniform rules, regulations, and requirements pertaining to the packaging of freight and the documentation of freight bills and interchange agreements; the development and dissemination of costing data; and the development and dissemination of business, economic, and financial projections.

21. The top four firms in the LTL sector increased their market share from 18.3 percent to 36.9 percent of total revenues between 1977 and 1987.

to comply with safety regulations, such as drivers' hours-of-service and licensing and vehicle inspections, and to curtail maintenance to sustain slim profit margins.[22] To address this issue one must analyze how safety performance under regulation compares with what it would have been under deregulation. Unfortunately, this counterfactual analysis cannot be carried out in a reliable way because we cannot unambiguously identify regulatory-induced accidents.[23]

Although not a counterfactual analysis, one study suggests that motor carriers operating before the passage of the Motor Carrier Act had accident rates in 1977 and 1984 that show no statistically significant difference.[24] A possible source of problems is carriers that came into existence after enactment of the Motor Carrier Act. These new entrants were found during 1985–86 to have a significantly higher accident rate than carriers that had been in business before deregulation.[25] But among these new entrants, only those carriers in business for less than two years had statistically higher accident rates than established carriers.[26] And it is not clear that these new entrants' safety records would have been better under regulation.

Although deregulation eased entry restrictions and thus may have increased the number of the unsafe new entrants, resurrecting entry barriers is not the appropriate policy to improve safety. Frequent and comprehen-

22. The effect of deregulation on safety in the rail industry has not emerged as a serious issue.

23. Including truck accidents that are unrelated to regulatory policy in a counterfactual analysis will add considerable noise to the statistical work and possibly produce biased results. The leading contributors to motor vehicle accidents (driver fatigue and resulting errors, vehicle deficiencies, traffic and road conditions, and vehicle speeds) have not changed during the change in regulatory policy. It is, therefore, difficult to identify a priori where regulatory policy has affected motor carrier safety. Several statistical analyses conducted with the objective of establishing a causal link between regulatory policy and motor vehicle safety have failed to establish a consistent link. U.S. Congress, Office of Technology Assessment, *Gearing Up for Safety: Motor Carrier Safety in a Competitive Environment*, OTA-SET-382 (Washington: U.S. Government Printing Office, September 1988), p.10; and Diane S. Owen, "Deregulation in the Trucking Industry," U.S. Federal Trade Commission, Bureau of Economics, May 1988, survey several of these studies.

24. Thomas M. Corsi, Philip Fanara, Jr., and Judith L. Jarrell, "Safety Performance of Pre-MCA Motor Carriers: 1977 Versus 1984," *Transportation Journal*, vol. 27 (Spring 1988), pp. 30–36.

25. Thomas M. Corsi and Philip Fanara, Jr., "Effects of New Entrants on Motor Carrier Safety," in Leon N. Moses and Ian Savage, eds., *Transportation Safety in an Age of Deregulation* (London: Oxford University Press, 1989), pp. 241–57.

26. Thomas M. Corsi and Philip Fanara, Jr., "Deregulation, New Entrants, and the Safety Learning Curve," *Journal of the Transportation Research Forum*, vol. 29, no. 1 (1988), pp. 3–8.

sive inspections of vehicles and their drivers would discourage the operation of deficient vehicles and crack down on drivers who violate hours-of-service regulations. Speed and weight limits should be more strictly enforced, and licensing of commercial drivers should also be more strict. Unsafe drivers should not be able to hide their poor driving record with multiple licenses. These policies would be especially effective because they would enhance the safety practices of new entrants.[27]

Recent public policy is moving in this direction. The Surface Transportation Assistance Act of 1982 established the Motor Carrier Safety Assistance Program (MCSAP), the cornerstone of which is a system of random roadside inspections of trucks by personnel from state and federal agencies. Subsequently, the Commercial Vehicle Safety Act of 1986 mandated a single national commercial driver's license and high standards to obtain one. Additionally, in 1988 Congress repealed the exemption from safety regulations that previously had existed for motor carriers operating within commercial zones of individual cities. These types of policies will be effective in the fight for safer trucking operations. Attempts to improve safety by regulating economic conduct will prove counterproductive.

Efficient Highway Pricing and Investment

The motor carrier industry has been hurt by ineffective government management of its infrastructure. Inefficient pricing of and investment in the nation's highways have wasted fuel, damaged trucks, and increased delivery times as congestion and disruptions due to road repairs have worsened. The cost to the motor carrier industry has been estimated in the billions.[28] Efficient highway pricing and investment would reduce these costs, enhance the use of technical advances in equipment and operations, and enable society to reap the full benefits of deregulation.

Conclusion

The success of surface freight deregulation to date suggests that no major policy initiatives are currently needed. But public policy can play

27. For further discussion of appropriate policy toward motor carrier safety, see the papers in Moses and Savage, *Transportation Safety in an Age of Deregulation*.

28. Kenneth A. Small, Clifford Winston, and Carol A. Evans, *Road Work: A New Highway Pricing and Investment Policy* (Brookings, 1989).

an important role in both the rail and motor carrier industries by continuing to promote competition and carrier efficiency and by preserving the gains already achieved. The failure of policymakers to do so in the airline industry has eroded some of the benefits from airline deregulation.[29] Public policy could play a major role in revitalizing the rail industry if the industry's performance takes a serious turn for the worse. In such a contingency the plan that we have outlined provides a basis for debating the merits of the radical possibility of separating track ownership from operation of the rails.

29. Steven A. Morrison and Clifford Winston, ''Airline Deregulation and Public Policy,'' *Science*, vol. 245 (August 1989), pp. 707–11.

Chapter Six

A Final Assessment

THE NATION'S surface freight transportation industry was deregulated to solve two distinct problems: excessive rates in the trucking industry, especially in the less-than-truckload sector, and insufficient returns on investment in the rail industry. Deregulation has contributed to solving both problems by allowing market forces to operate more freely.

Although further improvements in efficiency are expected as the railroad and motor carrier industries continue to adjust to the change in their regulatory environment, freight deregulation has already been a success. Conservatively estimated, it has generated $20 billion (1988 dollars) in annual benefits to shippers and their customers. These benefits grow directly out of the correction of distortions caused by regulation. Railroad regulation had little effect on entry, but it did distort the pattern of rates and the quality of service. In sharply reducing these distortions, deregulation did not benefit shippers and their customers by way of lower rates, which must come from a significant general increase in competition; indeed, under the conservative assumptions made here, rates, on average, rose slightly. Rather, it benefited shippers by promoting better service quality. In the case of trucking, regulation restricted both entry and service, with the result that deregulation brought about a general increase in competitiveness, a reduction in rates and costs, and an improvement in service.

Deregulation also forced the rail and motor carrier industries to become more innovative and efficient. In the process, the rail industry has gained $2.9 billion (1988 dollars) in annual profits from deregulation. Less-than-truckload trucking firms, facing increased competition, have lost $5.3 billion (1988 dollars) a year in profits. The labor force in the LTL sector has suffered wage and job losses, while that in the rail sector has suffered wage losses. Railroads gained from deregulation because regulation impeded cost-minimizing operations; LTL carriers and labor lost because regulation also impeded competition.

Although deregulation has made substantial progress in improving efficiency in freight transportation, shippers could gain an additional $5.6 billion (1977 dollars) if rail rates were forced, through increased competition, to marginal cost. These gains, however, would be at the expense of railroad profits, which, although substantially improved by deregulation, continue to be low. Because rail shippers' welfare and railroad profitability can improve and, in fact, have continued to do so in the years following the period of our analysis, policymakers should refrain from taking any dramatic measures to improve performance, but should continue to promote efficiency and competition among carriers. Different interest groups will, of course, continue to press for changes in policy, up to and including the restoration of regulation. Thus, it is crucial that policymakers not undermine support for deregulation by advancing policies inconsistent with its aims.

Index

American Trucking Association, 22n, 34n
Amtrak, 2
Association of American Railroads, 11, 19n, 24, 26, 30n, 31, 38n, 39–40, 46n, 49n
Atkinson, Scott E., 28n

Bailey, Elizabeth E., 1n
Bankruptcy: railroads, 3, 11; trucking industry, 12
Barbera, Anthony, 38n
Barnekov, Christopher C., 30n, 53n
Boyer, Kenneth D., 7, 25n, 30
Burlington Northern Railroad, 11, 54, 58n
Button, K. J., 51n

Canada, National Transportation Act of 1987, 57
Capacity, excess, of railroads, 13, 42, 52, 53
Cartelization, 7
Chessie (CSX), 11, 58n
Commercial Vehicle Safety Act of 1986, 63
Compensating variations, 16, 19–21, 44, 46–47
Competition: in railroads, 12, 44–49, 53–56; in trucking industry, 3, 4–5, 10, 11, 12–13, 28, 36–37, 61–62
Congress. See under names of specific legislation
Conrail, 3, 55, 58n
Corsi, Thomas M., 13n, 34n, 62n
Costs of regulation, 8–9
Counterfactual analysis, 15–16, 21, 31, 35, 62
CV. See Compensating variations

Daughety, Andrew F., 21n
Delaney, Robert V., 27n, 29–30
Deregulation: benefits to shippers, 5, 6, 49–50; effects on labor, 39–40; effects on railroads, 28, 30, 37–38, 50–51; effects on service to small communities, 40; effects on trucking industry, 27–28, 33–37; 7, 65; shipper optimality and, 43–44
Due, John F., 40n

Economic Recovery Tax Act of 1981, 38n
Employment and wages: of railroads, 9, 10, 11, 39–40, 65; of trucking industry, 39, 65
Eno Foundation for Transportation, 24n, 60n
Entry and exit regulations, 7–9, 10–11, 62–63
Evans, Carol A., 63n
Exit regulations. See Entry and exit regulations

Fanara, Philip, Jr., 62n
Federal Energy Regulatory Commission, 4n
4R Act. See Railroad Revitalization and Regulatory Reform Act
Friedlaender, Ann F., 33n, 43n

Government regulation: costs of, 8–9; market entry and exit, 7–8; of railroads, 1–3; of trucking industry, 3–5. See also Deregulation
Gradison, Heather, 11n
Griliches, Zvi, 21n
Grimm, Curtis M., 13n, 46n, 50n, 51n, 54n, 55n

Hamilton, Martha M., 60n
Harris, Robert G., 11n, 46n, 51n, 55n
Hepburn Act of 1906, 4n
Highways: efficient pricing and investment, 1, 63; interstate system development, 1, 4

ICC. See Interstate Commerce Commission
Inaba, Fred S., 21n
Inland water transport, 1
Intermodal operations, 13
Interstate Commerce Act of 1887, 1, 7
Interstate Commerce Commission (ICC), 13, 44–45, 46; creation of, 1; jurisdiction of, 4n; railroad abandonment and, 8, 10, 11; railroad competition and, 55; railroad mergers and, 27; railroad rates and, 2, 7, 9–10, 56; railroad regulation, 3, 49, 53; switching agreements under Staggers Act, 56; Toto Purchasing and Supply Company

DATE